ON THE
COALS

ON THE COALS

HEILIE PIENAAR

AUTHOR'S ACKNOWLEDGEMENTS

A project of this kind involves an enormous amount of time standing in smoke, tasting and eating, and an enormous amount of back-up from family and friends. To my parents in particular, thank you, I am deeply indebted. And special thanks to William for all the assistance and the many braais.

I am also most grateful to Mrs Thompson for opening her house for the photography, as well as Vickie from the Institute of Culinary Arts in Stellenbosch for assisting there. Also to Franz for the photography and to Best Duty for the use of the cast-iron pots.

And last, but not least, to those important people who made this book possible – Struik Publishers: Publishing manager Linda de Villiers, as well as Joy Clack, Beverley Dodd and Petal Palmer. Thank you for believing in me and for all your support.
Heilie Pienaar

Struik Publishers (Pty) Ltd
(a member of Struik New Holland Publishing (Pty) Ltd)
Cornelis Struik House
80 McKenzie Street
Cape Town 8001

Reg. No.: 54/00965/07

First published in 2000

10 9 8 7 6 5 4 3 2 1

Copyright © in published edition: Struik Publishers (Pty) Ltd 2000
Copyright © in text: Heilie Pienaar 2000
Copyright © in photographs: Struik Image Library/Franz Lauinger 2000

All rights reserved. No part of this publication may be reproduced, stored in a retrieval system, or transmitted, in any form or by any means, electronic, mechanical, photocopying, recording or otherwise, without the prior written permission of the copyright owner/s.

PUBLISHING MANAGER: Linda de Villiers
EDITOR: Joy Clack
CONCEPT DESIGNER: Petal Palmer
DESIGNER: Beverley Dodd
PHOTOGRAPHER: Franz Lauinger
STYLIST: Heilie Pienaar
PROOFREADER: Proofread cc
INDEXER: Brenda Brickman

Reproduction by Hirt & Carter Cape (Pty) Ltd
Printed and bound by Sino Publishing, Hong Kong

ISBN 1 86872 391 7

contents

introduction 6

marinades, bastes & glazes 18
  marinades 18
  bastes 22
  glazes 23

snacks 24

meat 32
  beef & veal 32
  mutton & lamb 42
  pork 50
  venison 58

fish & seafood 60

poultry 68

potjie 76

spit-roast 86

accompaniments 90
  breads 90
  vegetables 96
  salads & dressings 100

desserts 104

index 111

introduction

Cooking over coals has been done for many years, and although the technique remains the same, we now have more interesting ingredients available, such as peppadews and sun-dried tomatoes. All the recipes included in this book are quick and easy and will appeal to even the most inexperienced braaier. Make sure you have all equipment at hand to avoid last-minute dashes from kitchen to braai.

Two types of braais are available – charcoal/wood or gas/electric – but the principle remains the same. Food is placed on a grid over heat and the fat and cooking juices are released onto the hot coals. The ensuing aroma-filled smoke/steam combination is absorbed, contributing to the distinctive character of braaied food.

Wood or charcoal braai

It is worthwhile buying a good quality braai as it will last longer. If it is portable, try to store it in a protected place. Choose a braai that offers cooking space for the number of people you cater for on a regular basis. The holes in the grid or rack should not be too big as food will fall through. A wide variety of braais are available, from inexpensive disposable trays to expensive sophisticated models.

BUILT-IN BRAAI
This is a permanent feature which is usually either attached to a house or is free-standing and located in the garden or on the patio. It consists of a three-sided wall with strong metal pegs which support a solid plate for the coals. It is advisable to have multiple levels above the coals at which the grid can be placed to enable the distance from the coals to be varied.

UPRIGHT OPEN BRAAI
Normally consisting of a braai surface supported by four legs, these braais also come with wheels. They are easy to use and can be cleaned easily. They are not always a long-term investment as they are usually made of thin steel, but if covered and protected from inclement weather, they should last much longer. These braais vary in size and are ideal for cooking small items, such as sausages or burgers.

BARREL BRAAI
This attractive, steady, open-style braai (usually a half-drum or gas cylinder) has a large braaiing surface for a large amount of meat. They usually have adjustable cooking heights and a spit-braai can often be incorporated.

DISPOSABLE BRAAIS WITH CHARCOAL
Readily available in most supermarkets, this braai consists of a grid and shallow foil tray, pre-filled with charcoal and a firelighter. It is ideal for taking on a picnic or to use on a tiny balcony or patio, and can be placed on the ground or any heat-resistant surface. The rack is very close to the coals, making it ideal for cooking small items, such as chops and sausages.

KETTLE BRAAI (WEBER BRAAI)
Various sizes are available, from tabletop portables, which are ideal for picnics or balconies, to free-standing models. The rounded shape and lid reflects the heat from all surfaces and cooks the food evenly, reducing the cooking time, sealing in the juices and giving the food a smoky flavour. The cover helps keep out oxygen, which reduces flare-ups, and also keeps the smoke inside, intensifying the smoked effect. Covered kettle braais enable longer cooking for large cuts of meat and whole birds without drying them out. Kettle braais seldom rust or burn through as they are made of enamel-coated, heavy-gauge steel.

CLOCKWISE FROM TOP LEFT: *Portable braais – Galvanized braai, Kettle braai, Double braai with potjie hook, Upright open braai, Gas braai (skottelbraai).*

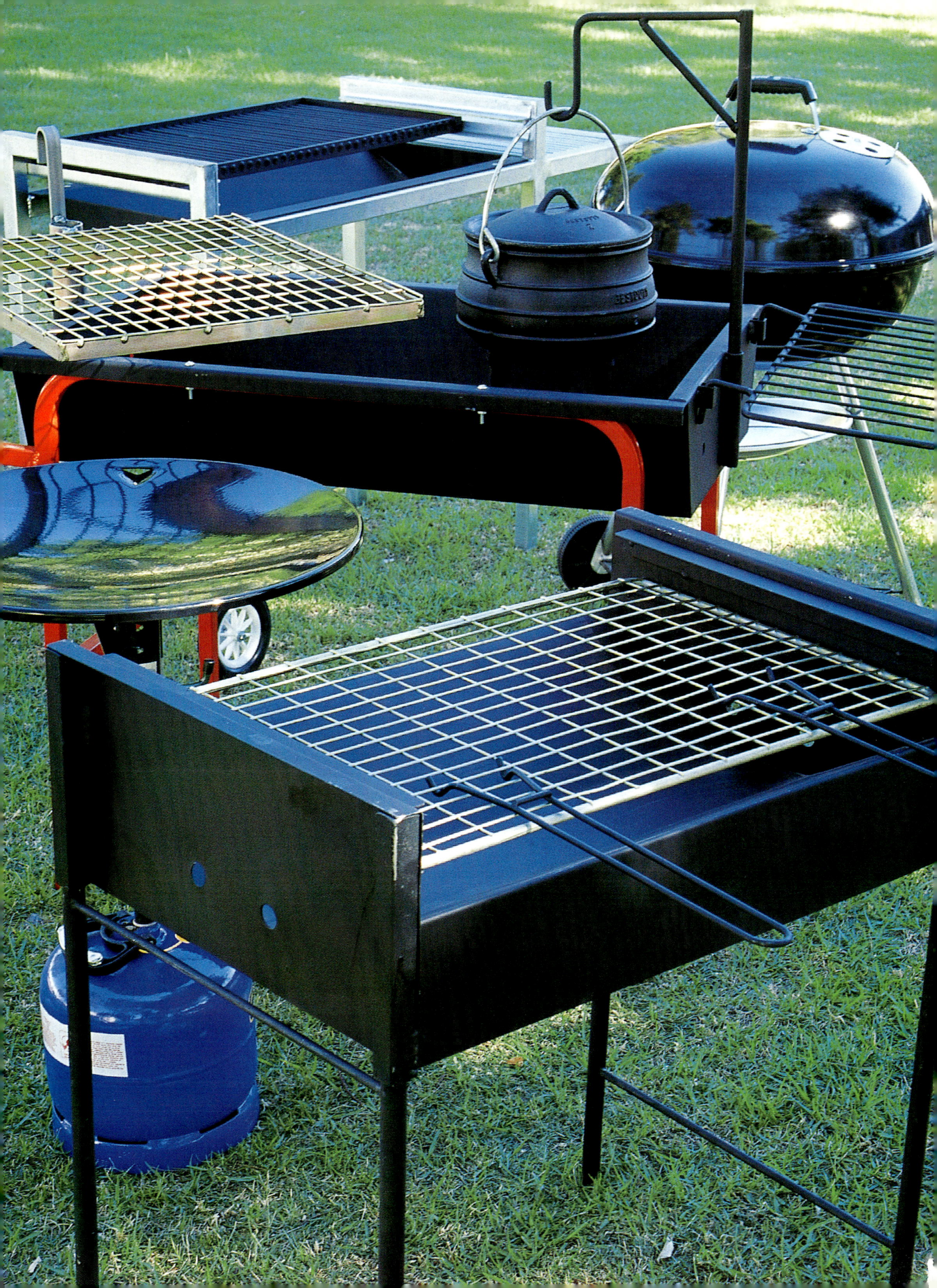

With a kettle braai you can cook food in two ways:

Direct cooking method – Best-suited to tender food that cooks quickly, such as small pieces of meat, steaks or fish. Coals are placed across the entire charcoal grill area underneath the meat.

Indirect cooking method – Best-suited to large cuts of meat, such as roasts, whole birds or whole fish. The food is cooked by reflected heat as well as heat from the coals, which are placed along the sides of the kettle, behind two charcoal rails.

A special smoked flavour can be induced by adding any of a variety of wood shaving mixtures (see page 11). A meat thermometer is useful to check the internal temperature of large cuts. Refer to the manual supplied with the braai to check cooking temperatures for the different cuts of meat.

Gas braai and electric braai

These braais can be preheated within 10 minutes. Individual controls for each burner offer more versatility and the heat is easy to regulate, giving control over the cooking process. You also don't have the inconvenience of messy ashes. Small gas braais are convenient, quick and ideal for outdoors, such as picnics. Gas and electric braais, however, do not create the same ambiance as a wood braai.

Fuels

The secret of a successful braai is a good fire that will produce hot coals, which will not burn out before the food is cooked. The art of controlling the heat and distributing it evenly becomes easy with practice.

COALS

Coals can be produced from wood or charcoal and are available in bags from most cafés and supermarkets.

WOOD

Many people prefer wood rather than charcoal as the smoke imparts a distinctive flavour to the food. Buy wood and store it until dry enough to use. Dry hardwood is ideal for a good braai. Different woods are available and can be purchased in stores or along the roadside outside the cities. These include hard-coal, red bush, camel-thorn, umbrella thorn, sickle-bush and Rooikrans, or even vine stumps (mostly from the Western Province). You can also use wood from fruit trees, such as fig and plum, as they produce excellent coals.

Smoke from pine, certain types of gum trees, and wood that has been painted, sealed or treated with any chemicals, gives food an unpleasant flavour.

Never use wood from Tamboti or Oleander trees – it is poisonous.

CHARCOAL AND BRIQUETTES

Two types are commonly available – natural charcoal chips and briquettes. Both burn quicker than wood and are ideal if you are pressed for time. Briquettes are oval-shaped lumps of compressed charcoal, made from particles of waste charcoal mixed with a starch binder. Once lit, these tend to burn longer than charcoal chips.

FIRELIGHTERS

Many people find firelighters indispensable for starting fires easily. They are also clean and easy to use. Small pieces can be broken off and placed between the charcoal or briquettes. Firelighters are available from almost all cafés and supermarkets.

FIRELIGHTER FLUID

Sold in a bottle. Take care when using firelighter fluid as it can cause the fire to flare up.

Preparing the fire

Allow at least 45 minutes to 1 hour for wood or charcoal coals to reach the heat required for most braais. There are different ways of making fires and everyone has their own way. The basics, however, remain the same. Place a firelighter and light it, then pack the wood in criss-cross fashion over it, or scoop charcoal chips or briquettes into a pyramid shape over it. You could also use a charcoal starter (available from supermarkets). Leave the fire to burn until the coals begin to glow. Once the coals are ready – there should be no flames and the coals should be a light grey ashy colour (red at night) – spread them over the base of the braai. If a large quantity of meat is being cooked, have a small fire going on the side to provide extra coals when required.

Never light a fire with paraffin or petrol, as this is extremely dangerous, will impart a terrible smell and will taint the food.

CLOCKWISE FROM LEFT: *Camel-thorn, charcoal starter, briquettes, Rooikrans, charcoal, basting brush, tongs, firelighters*

Judging the correct temperature of the coals

HOT
The flames will have disappeared and the coals will glow red, barely covered with ash. You should be able to hold your hand about 100 mm above the coals for 2–3 seconds. A hot fire is used for tender meat, such as steak, as well as fish and small pieces of chicken or meat that do not require long braaiing.

MODERATE OR MEDIUM-HOT
Most of the redness in the coals will have disappeared and the coals will glow through a layer of grey ash. Thick white ash will also be visible. You should be able to hold your hand above the coals for 4–5 seconds. This temperature is used for most braais – sausages, chops, vegetables, etc.

LOW
The coals will no longer be red and will be covered with a thick layer of grey ash. You should be able to hold your hand over the coals for approximately 6–7 seconds. This temperature is not often used, except where indicated in the recipes.

CONTROLLING THE HEAT OF COALS
First try moving the grid to a lower or higher position. To increase the heat of the fire, knock or blow some excess ash off the coals and move them closer together. New coals, prepared alongside, can also be added. To decrease the heat, spread the coals further apart and allow them to burn down for 5–10 minutes longer.

Care of grid

The braai should cool down completely before it can be cleaned. Remove cold ashes from the hearth and brush out dust. Remove the grid and scrub it with a brass brush. For burned-on grease, use an oven cleaner, following the manufacturer's directions, then rinse and dry.

Choosing meat to braai

Good quality meat will result in a good end product. The grilling process will not transform inferior quality meat into a masterpiece. Meat needs to be matured before use, as although it may be of good quality, it can still be tough. Maturing is a natural process which tenderizes beef and lamb (pork is tender enough). Beef can be ripened at home in the refrigerator for 7–10 days, lamb for 2–5 days.

Methods of cooking

DRY HEAT (DIRECT)

Tender meat is cooked in this way. Food is placed on a grid directly over the coals and is then turned to cook it on both sides. Food can be cooked over the hottest part of the fire and then moved to the side to finish cooking. Average cooking times are given in the recipes.

MOIST HEAT (INDIRECT)

Less tender cuts are done this way. Liquid is often added to make the meat more tender, for example when making a potjie. Food can also be cooked in a kettle braai with the lid on – although the heat is restricted to the sides, it is reflected from all sides. This is ideal for cooking larger cuts of meat and whole birds.

Braai safety

- Never use petrol or lighting fuel directly on the fire.
- Never move a lit braai.
- Keep a fire extinguisher handy in case the fire gets out of control.
- Keep a spray bottle of water handy in case of flare-ups.
- Wait until ashes are cold before disposing of them carefully.
- Keep your eye on the braai at all times. This is essential for safety reasons.
- Use long-handled cooking tools and oven gloves.

Braai utensils

TONGS

Long metal tongs, preferably with wooden handles, are absolutely essential for turning meat on the braai. A fork is not ideal to use as the sharp prongs can damage the meat fibres and allow valuable juices to escape, making the meat tough.

BASTING BRUSH

Wide, long-handled brushes are preferable. A paint brush can also be used if it is kept exclusively for the braai. Avoid nylon-bristled brushes as the heat from the fire will melt the bristles and ruin the meat.

SKEWERS

Metal skewers conduct heat well and are therefore mostly used for heavier cuts of food that require longer cooking times such as kebabs, spatchcocked poultry and butterflied pieces. They also ensure even cooking.

Wooden and bamboo skewers are ideal for smaller, delicate foods such fish, chicken and vegetables. Soak the skewers in water for 30 minutes prior to braaiing to prevent them from burning.

Cooking times

Use the times given in the individual recipes as a guideline, but take note of the food, not the clock! Only approximate times can be given for meat cooked on a braai, so prepare food to your personal taste.

The length of time taken for meat to be cooked depends on a number of factors: the kind of meat (beef, pork, lamb, poultry, fish or venison), the thickness of the cut, the temperature of the coals, and the distance of the meat from the coals. Take care not to overcook meat as it will become dry and tough.

Place chops or steak 50–100 mm from the coals. Thicker cuts should be placed 100–150 mm from the coals.

Also consider the order in which the different types of meat should be cooked. Sausages, hamburgers, chicken and spare ribs can be kept warm without spoiling and can therefore be cooked first. Steak, chops, sosaties or kebabs and fish taste better if served straight from the fire.

For larger cuts of meat, such as leg of lamb on the spit, remove from fire and allow to rest in a warm place for 10–15 minutes while the juices are absorbed.

Smoking

Smoking as a cooking method is where meat is cooked whilst being smoked. In a kettle braai the food gets a wonderfully smoky aroma and flavour. For smoking, add soaked wood chips or pieces to hot coals during cooking. Wood pieces can be used dry but are normally soaked in water for about 30 minutes. Soak large pieces longer. Shake off excess water before adding to coals.

SAWDUST

Different types of wood impart their own unique flavour. Use only hard, non-resinous woods, such as mesquite, walnut, oak, peach, pear or apple. The sawdust must be completely dry or it will not smoulder. For extra flavour, soak herbs in water for 10 minutes, drain and sprinkle over the sawdust.

Resinous woods such as pine should not be used as they could lead to stomach disorders and will give meat an unpleasant taste.

Aromatics

The flavour of braaied food can be improved naturally or by adding manufactured flavourings to the fire during the cooking process.

When the fire is hot enough for cooking, place fresh herbs, dry twigs from herbs or fruit trees, such as thyme, rosemary, bay leaves or lemon, on the coals. Seaweed can also be used to impart a special flavour, as can nut shells, such as almond and walnut. Soak them in water for about 30 minutes, drain and then sprinkle onto the coals.

Potjies

A potjie is a way of cooking meals in a three-legged or flat cast-iron pot. Potjies that do not require curing or special preparation before use are available these days. After use, wash the pot with soap and water and rinse well. Dry the pot thoroughly, then wipe it with a paper towel and cooking oil before storing it in a dry place. This will keep it in good condition and will prevent rust. If traces of rust do appear, remove them by rubbing lightly with fine-grained sandpaper or coarse salt. Wipe over with oil again.

Three-legged potjies are available in various sizes. The lower the number, the smaller the pot. They are used for the more traditional layered potjie.

Flat-base potjies are also available in various sizes and are usually used for breads, casseroles or stir-fries.

Tips for making a potjie

- Heat the potjie first. Add oil and brown the meat in batches. Add liquid, close pot tightly with lid. It must simmer, not boil.
- Add vegetables in layers 30 minutes before serving. Large or hard vegetables that take longer to cook should be added first and smaller or softer ones placed on top.
- Rice can be added in the centre between vegetable layers (on the side it can easily burn). When cooking rice, more liquid is required: 2 cups (500 ml) liquid to each cup (250 ml) of rice. Replace lid and simmer for 30 minutes.

THE FIRE FOR A POTJIE

Moderate, even heat is important. To achieve this, make sure that low-heat coals are evenly distributed under the potjie. To prevent food from burning, place the pot on bricks or on a metal three-legged stand, which prevents the pot from standing directly in the coals. The pot can also be hung from a hook above the fire and can be used on gas cylinders as well, although a special attachment is required for this (available from camping outlets).

INGREDIENTS

Meat

More economical cuts can be used as the long cooking process helps to soften and moisten less tender cuts.

Liquid

Do not add too much liquid, as most of the moisture will be retained if the lid is kept on. If necessary, you can always add more liquid at a later stage. Use meat stock, wine, fruit juice, sherry or beer. Water will not contribute to the flavour.

Vegetables

Onions and garlic are essential ingredients in a potjie. Because it is difficult to thicken sauce when the pot is full, potatoes are commonly used as a thickener. It is preferable to use fresh vegetables rather than frozen or canned, and keep in mind that whole vegetables take longer to cook than sliced or smaller cuts.

Beef

The secret of braaiing beef successfully is to use well-matured meat from a young, well-fed animal. The longer the meat is grilled, the more flavour and succulence it loses.

Veal is normally produced in smaller quantities. It comes from calves up to five months old and weighing no more than 90–110 kg. The meat is always tender, as the calf's connective tissue has not yet toughened. It has a delicate flavour, with low fat and high moisture content.

QUALITY CHARACTERISTICS

Colour: Good quality beef has a cherry-red colour. Older beef is darker red in colour.
Texture: The meat should be firm to the touch.
Fat: It should be firm and evenly distributed over the carcass.

RECOMMENDED TIMING

A minimum thickness of 25 mm is recommended for steaks grilled over hot coals. This will ensure juicier and moister meat. Rare to medium-done is recommended.

Steaks
Rare:	25 mm thick (6–8 minutes)
	35 mm thick (8–10 minutes)
Medium-done:	25 mm thick (10–12 minutes)
	35 mm thick (12–15 minutes)
Well-done:	25 mm thick (15–18 minutes)
Kebabs	25 mm thick (12–15 minutes)

Lamb

Nothing can compare with the flavour of lamb over the coals. Being very versatile, it can be braaied as chops, ribs, sosaties or whole on a spit.

Mutton and lamb differ from each other in that lambs are slaughtered very young, therefore the meat is very tender. Mutton, having more connective tissue than lamb, is less tender but more tasty. It can become more tender when cooked using moist heat.

QUALITY CHARACTERISTICS

Colour: Good quality lamb has a bright pink colour, while mutton is slightly darker.
Texture: The meat should be firm to the touch. Lamb has a finer texture than mutton.
Fat: It should be firm and evenly distributed over the carcass.

RECOMMENDED TIMING

A minimum thickness of 20 mm is recommended for chops grilled over moderate coals. This will ensure juicier and moister meat. Medium-done is recommended.

Leg	butterflied thickness varies (1¼ hours)
Chops	20 mm thick (12–14 minutes)
Kebabs	20 mm thick (10–15 minutes)

Pork

Pigs are usually slaughtered at 8 months, and therefore the meat is tender and makes excellent roasts. It contains less fat than red meat and is a good choice for a lower fat intake.

QUALITY CHARACTERISTICS

Colour: The meat of a young animal is greyish-pink. Older animals have darker meat.
Texture: The meat and fat should feel firm to the touch.
Fat: It should be white to creamy white in colour.

RIND

Always remove the rind when applying moist heat cooking methods or when meat is to be marinated or basted. Pork rind becomes very tough when in contact with moisture.

To prepare crackling: Score rind in diamond shape, rub in oil and salt mixture, bake at 160 °C (325 °F) for 25 minutes per 500 g and the last 30 minutes at 200 °C (400 °F).

RECOMMENDED TIMING

A minimum thickness of 20 mm is recommended for chops grilled over moderate coals. This will ensure juicier and moister meat. Medium- to well-done is recommended.

Leg	butterflied thickness varies (1¼ hours)
Chops	20 mm thick (16–20 minutes)
Kebabs	20 mm thick (12–15 minutes)

Venison

In South Africa we are familiar with springbok, blesbok, impala and kudu, which are commonly available in retail butcheries during winter. Venison is very lean and larding for certain cuts is recommended. As with beef, the age of the animal affects the tenderness. The forequarter cuts are best cooked using moist heat methods. Venison needs correct preparation and cooking to bring out the best flavour.

MARINATING

Traditionally, venison is marinated with wine, vinegar or lemon juice to help tenderize it and tone down the flavour. Red wine marinade is a firm favourite, but be careful not to overwhelm the venison by adding too much red wine. Yoghurt or beer marinades can also be used. If the marinade is to be used for cooking after marinating, add a bit of water to prevent the sauce from being too sour.

COOKING METHODS FOR VENISON

Dry heat – braai (grill): For the most tender cuts, indirect or dry heat is applied and no liquid is required.
Moist heat – potjie: For the less tender cuts, liquid is required to tenderize the meat.

Poultry

This includes chicken, turkey, duck, ostrich and the less commonly used goose, guinea fowl and quail.

There are many ways to prepare poultry – whole, halved, spatchcocked, cut into pieces, on the bone, off the bone or stuffed. Do not overcook poultry as it will become dry and tasteless.

Chicken

Fresh chicken has a superior flavour and texture compared with frozen. The skin should be moist and the breast plump and well rounded. Free-range birds are recommended as they are reared outdoors and their flavour is superior to intensively-reared birds. Chickens weigh about 1.5 kg and usually serve four. Baby chickens (or poussins) weigh about

CLOCKWISE FROM TOP LEFT: *Lamb saddle, lamb chump chops, chicken portions, boerewors, pork fillet, pork rashers, pork chops, Porterhouse steak, T-bone steak, lamb riblets, lamb loin chop*

introduction 13

500 g and are enough for one person. After purchasing, refrigerate or freeze chicken as soon as possible.

Cooking times will depend on the thickness of the pieces. Keep in mind that boneless cuts will cook more quickly than whole birds. Chicken does not need to be tenderized, but marinades will add extra flavour. White wine marinades are best. Marinate for a short time and turn frequently.

Chicken must always be thoroughly cooked before it can be eaten. Be careful, however, not to overcook it as the meat will become very dry. To test whether it is ready, insert a skewer into the thickest part of the meat – when the juices run clear, the chicken is done.

RECOMMENDED TIMING:
Drumsticks/thighs 15–20 minutes
Whole in kettle braai 1 hour
Chicken kebabs 10–12 minutes

Turkey

A full-grown turkey can weigh over 9 kg, and is sold fresh, frozen or in portions. Self-basting turkeys, pre-injected with butter or oil under the skin, are also available. When choosing a turkey, check that the skin is clean and does not have any blemishes or bruises. Fresh or defrosted birds should also have a pleasant smell. Covered turkeys can be stored in the refrigerator for up to four days. Because turkey meat is fairly dry, it needs to be brushed constantly with oil and should be wrapped in foil to prevent it from drying out.

Duck

Ducks are sold either fresh or frozen. Most ducks are actually ducklings with a mass that varies from 1–3.2 kg. Duck has a lot of bone and fat in proportion to its size, therefore allow at least 450 g per person. Frozen ducks are available all year round – look for a plump, meaty breast and unblemished skin. Covered, ducks can be stored in the refrigerator for 2–3 days.

Frozen duck must be thoroughly defrosted, preferably in the refrigerator, before cooking. Prick the skin with a needle or fork beforehand for excess fat to drain out during the cooking process. Whole duck is usually roasted, while portions can be used in moist heat cooking. When roasting, baste with your favourite marinade or any of the following: honey, orange juice, brandy, ginger, bacon, garlic, pineapple or berries.

Fish

Fish is very versatile and tasty done over coals. It is important to prepare and cook it correctly to keep the flesh moist and to produce a better flavour.

Fish can be divided into two categories, namely oily and white fish. Oily fish (snoek, galjoen, mackerel, elf, tunny, swordfish, yellowtail, barracuda) retains moisture naturally and does not require constant basting as with white fish (hake, silvers, kingklip, kabeljou (kob), stumpnose, Cape salmon (geelbek), red Roman, steenbras, Hottentot, blue fish, angelfish, musselcracker, sole, monkfish, John Dory).

PURCHASING FRESH FISH
Fish should not have a strong fish smell. It should be firm to the touch, with a wet and shiny appearance. Whole fish should have red or pink gills and clear and slightly bulging eyes; fillets, steaks and shrimp should have shiny surfaces; clams and oysters should have tightly closed shells. It is best to buy fresh fish. Frozen fish is not really suitable for grilling as it loses about 30% of its moisture as it thaws. It should therefore be prepared using moist cooking methods. Fresh fish should be braaied immediately.

PREPARING FISH
Immediately after fish has been caught, cut off its head and drain the blood to improve the flavour. Cut along the belly and clip off the gills. Remove entrails and rinse well. To scale a fish, hold it by the tail and scrape with the back of a knife, working down towards the head. Rinse under running water. To fillet fish, cut along the backbone from head to tail. The whole bone will now be visible. Start at the tail end, cut the flesh away from the bone, turn to the other side and repeat. Cut fillets away.

A FEW WAYS TO TEST IF FISH IS DONE
Leave fish on the grill long enough for the skin to brown and pull away from the grill before trying to turn it. It should lift easily and cleanly. Grill fish until it is opaque through the thickest part. The flesh should flake easily. Whole fish is cooked when the tail becomes loose and the eyes turn white.

RECOMMENDED TIMING:
Mostly moderate heat 100 mm from coals.
Whole fish, ± 800 g 25–30 minutes
Fillet steaks, 25 mm thick 10–12 minutes

Beef – most suitable cuts

FOREQUARTER
The meat is less tender, but very tasty. If handled correctly, such as marinating, cooking slowly and using indirect cooking method (such as potjie or kettle), these cuts can be just as successful for braaiing as the hindquarter cuts (mostly steaks).

Primary cuts	Smaller cuts	Cooking method
NECK, SHIN & CHUCK (large % of bone)	cubed or sliced	potjie
FLAT RIB (flat shape with ribs)	deboned and rolled, marinated	potjie
PRIME RIB (cut into thick slices)	with bone – prime rib steaks deboned – scotch fillet steaks deboned and rolled	braai braai spit-roast and kettle braai

HINDQUARTER
This section contains the most tender cuts and is therefore ideal for braaiing using the direct heat cooking method. Most steaks are cut from the hindquarter.

Primary cuts	Smaller cuts	Cooking method
SHORT RIB (mostly rib)	whole or portions	potjie
WING RIB (large eye muscle with ribs)	deboned and rolled club and scotch fillet steaks	spit-roast and kettle braai braai
SIRLOIN (no ribs, T-shaped bone)	T-bone steaks Porterhouse	braai braai and kettle braai
RUMP (tender cut, contains part fillet)	debone, keep large rumpsteaks	grill and kettle braai braai
FILLET (boneless and most tender)	keep whole several fillet steaks – fillet minute, fillet mignon, fillet piccata, fillet tournedos	braai braai
TOPSIDE & SILVERSIDE	sliced and cubed	potjie
THICK FLANK	cubed and sliced	potjie

Lamb – most suitable cuts

Primary cuts	Smaller cuts	Cooking method
NECK (removed whole from carcass)	sliced	potjie
SHOULDER BLADE (contains blade, marrow and shin bone)	debone to butterfly	braai
FLANK AND BREAST (coarse texture)	cubed	potjie
RIB (rib bones with eye muscle)	deboned and rolled chops or cutlets	braai braai
LOIN (T-bone shape – fillet and large eye muscle) (deboned rolled loin, cut 25 mm thick) (eye muscle only, cut 25 mm thick)	deboned and rolled loin chops saratoga chops noisettes	spit-roast and kettle braai braai braai braai
SADDLE (loin and rib)	whole saddle chops	braai and kettle braai braai
CHUMP (pelvic bone and several muscle layers)	chops	braai
LEG (pelvic bone, marrow bone and shank bone)	whole, deboned and rolled cubed – sosaties, kebabs	spit-roast and kettle braai braai

Pork – most suitable cuts

Primary cuts	Smaller cuts	Cooking method
NECK	deboned and rolled	spit-roast and kettle braai
BELLY (thin boneless muscle and fat layer)	strips – kebabs	braai
BREAST (breast bone, rib bones and part of marrow bone)	spare ribs – marinated strips – kebabs	braai braai
THICK RIB (shoulder blade and few ribs)	chops deboned and cubed – kebabs	braai braai
RIB (eye muscle and few rib bones, vertebrae and even fat layer)	whole, deboned and rolled chops	kettle braai braai
LOIN (T-bone shape – fillet and large eye muscle) (deboned rolled loin, cut 25 mm thick) (eye muscle only, cut 25 mm thick)	deboned and rolled loin chops saratoga chops noisettes	spit-roast and kettle braai braai braai braai
CHUMP (several muscle layers and the pelvic bone)	chops	braai
LEG (marrow bone and several muscle layers)	with or without bone strips and cubed – kebabs	spit-roast and kettle braai braai

Venison – most suitable cuts

Primary cuts	Smaller cuts	Cooking method
NECK	sliced or cubed	potjie
SHOULDER AND CHUCK	whole, deboned and rolled cubed	potjie potjie
FLANK AND BRISKET	deboned and rolled cubed	potjie potjie
SADDLE (loin and rib)	whole saddle chops divided and cut rib and loin chops	potjie, spit-roast and kettle braai braai braai
LEG AND RUMP	whole, deboned and rolled smaller cuts for roasts thin slices for schnitzels	potjie, spit-roast and kettle braai potjie, spit-roast and kettle braai braai

General braai hints

- Buy matured meat, especially beef, for maximum tenderness.
- All cuts suitable for grilling are suitable for braaiing. With a braai, the meat actually grills over the coals.
- Allow 200–400 g meat per person, depending on appetite. This includes the weight of the bone. Allow less for boneless cuts like sausages and sosaties.
- Thaw meat beforehand in the refrigerator and have it ready at room temperature. Remove from freezer a day in advance. Quick thawing leads to greater moisture loss and results in dry and tough meat.
- Remove excess fat – dripping fat causes flare-ups. Slash fat ends at 25 mm intervals to prevent the meat from curling during cooking (especially pork chops).
- Only sprinkle on salt at the end of the cooking time and before serving as it draws out the juices, resulting in tough meat.
- Seasoning and marinades should improve the flavour of meat, not overpower it.
- Wipe excess marinade from meat with paper towel. Marinade can make the meat too dark, and moist meat does not brown well.
- Brush the grid with a little oil before braaiing to prevent food from sticking. This is not necessary for marinated meats.
- Grill steaks and chops 100 mm above the coals. Sausages and sosaties must be placed higher as they have to be grilled slowly.
- Use meat tongs to turn meat. Avoid sharp utensils such as forks, as this damages the meat fibres and causes loss of meat juices.
- Beef – Rare to medium-done is recommended.
- Lamb and pork – Medium- to well-done.
- Serve meat immediately since it toughens quickly.

marinades, bastes & glazes

marinades

Marinades serve multiple purposes: they tenderize the less tender cuts of meat, enhance the flavour and improve the appearance of the food before and during cooking. Marinades also ensure that meat is sufficiently moistened during cooking, especially if it is basted regularly.

Precise measuring is not absolutely necessary, as many marinades can be easily adapted to personal taste. Most marinades can also be made in advance and refrigerated for up to a week.

Marinades are usually made up of oil (you can use either cooking or olive oil), acid (vinegar, lemon juice or wine) and spices and herbs (for flavour). The general rule is one part oil to three parts liquid. Herbs and spices can be adjusted to taste.

If marinades with high sugar levels are used, such as honey or jams, grill slowly to prevent burning.

Use left-over marinade to prepare sauces or for basting the meat during the cooking process.

Key points on marinating

OIL

Use cooking or olive oil sparingly in marinades. Oil prevents the meat from becoming dry and adds moisture to lean meat, but too much will cause coals to flare up. Use flavoured oils as an alternative.

ACID

The acid element of a marinade is the one responsible for tenderizing the meat. Acid ingredients include lemon juice, wine, vinegar or acidic fruit juices (such as paw-paw, pineapple, orange).

OTHER INGREDIENTS

Use alcohol, such as sherry, or meat stock for more subtle and delicately flavoured marinade. Herbs add extra flavour. Use sprigs of fresh herbs if possible. Spices that can be used include mustard seeds, black pepper, garlic or root ginger.

Containers

Use a large glass or plastic container (metal can react with the acid in marinades) so that food can be turned easily. If the food is not completely submerged in the marinade, it should be turned halfway through the marinating time.

Large freezer bags also work well to marinate food. Add the food and marinade, seal and shake, and leave in the refrigerator for the required time, shaking occasionally.

Timing

It is preferable to marinate meat in the refrigerator, especially if it requires a long marinating time, but to speed up the process, it can be marinated at room temperature for about 30 minutes. Tender cuts, such as fillet and fish, should only be marinated for a maximum of 30 minutes. Smaller cuts, such as steaks, chops and kebabs can be marinated for 2–3 hours in the refrigerator. Larger meat cuts can be marinated for 4–6 hours in the refrigerator, or overnight if preferred. Making shallow cuts in the surface will enable the marinade to penetrate more easily.

CLOCKWISE FROM TOP LEFT: *Beer Marinade, Barbecue Marinade, Pineapple Glaze, Honey Glaze, Rosemary Baste, Yoghurt marinade (see pages 20–23)*

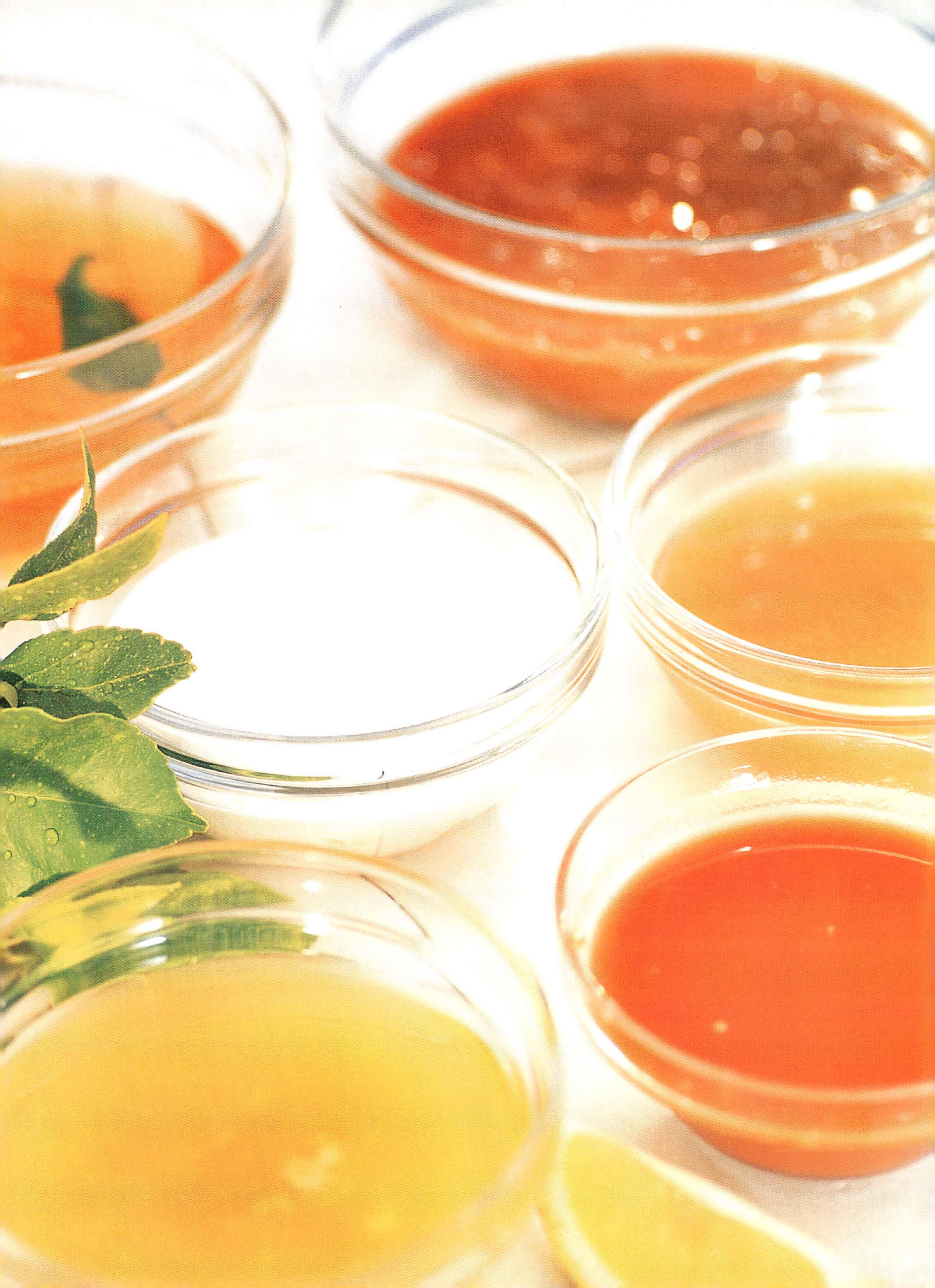

Deboned leg of lamb in basic marinade with wine (see page 21).

20 on the coals

BARBECUE MARINADE

This standard barbecue marinade is always popular and can be used for meat, poultry and fish.

30 ml (2 tbsp) butter
1 medium onion, chopped
2 cloves garlic, crushed
45 ml (3 tbsp) light brown sugar
60 ml (¼ cup) vinegar
5 ml (1 tsp) mustard powder
125 ml (½ cup) tomato sauce
125 ml (½ cup) water
15 ml (1 tbsp) Worcestershire sauce
15 ml (1 tbsp) fresh lemon juice
salt and freshly ground black pepper to taste

1. Heat butter in a heavy-based saucepan.
2. Sauté onion and garlic until soft.
3. Add all remaining ingredients and simmer for about 20 minutes. Cool before using.

YOGHURT MARINADE

Great with chicken, lamb or fish.

250 ml (1 cup) plain, unflavoured yoghurt
15 ml (1 tbsp) fresh lemon juice
15 ml (1 tbsp) chopped root ginger
2 cloves garlic, crushed
salt and freshly ground black pepper to taste

1. Mix all ingredients together and pour over meat.

SPICY ORIENTAL MARINADE

250 ml (1 cup) buttermilk or sour cream
15 ml (1 tbsp) fresh lemon juice
15 ml (1 tbsp) chopped root ginger
2 cloves garlic, crushed
2 ml (¼ tsp) chilli powder
5 ml (1 tsp) ground cumin
salt and freshly ground black pepper to taste

1. Mix all ingredients together and pour over meat.

BASIC MARINADE WITH WINE

Use white wine for chicken and fish, and red for lamb and beef.

125 ml (½ cup) dry white or red wine
80 ml (⅓ cup) olive oil
15 ml (1 tbsp) fresh lemon juice
2 ml (¼ tsp) grated lemon rind
1 bay leaf
15 ml (1 tbsp) freshly chopped thyme
or 5 ml (1 tsp) dried
2 cloves garlic, crushed

1. Mix all ingredients together and pour over meat.

LEMON AND HERB MARINADE

Ideal with chicken, pork, fish and lamb. Fresh herbs such as thyme or rosemary can also be used.

125 ml (½ cup) fresh lemon juice
2 ml (¼ tsp) grated lemon rind
60 ml (¼ cup) olive oil
15 ml (1 tbsp) chopped fresh origanum
or 5 ml (1 tsp) dried
10 ml (2 tsp) honey
2 cloves garlic, crushed
salt and freshly ground black pepper to taste

1. Mix all ingredients together and pour over meat.

BEER MARINADE

This one really tenderizes less tender meat cuts, such as beef or venison.

340 ml (1 can) beer
60 ml (¼ cup) olive oil
15 ml (1 tbsp) light brown sugar
30 ml (2 tbsp) fresh lemon juice
2 ml (¼ tsp) grated lemon rind
1 bay leaf
salt and freshly ground black pepper to taste

1. Mix all ingredients together and pour over meat.

bastes

The main purpose of a baste is to enhance the flavour, keep meat moist and to help glaze it. Most bastes contain herbs and/or acids such as red wine, buttermilk or fruit.

Basting is done by brushing food with flavoured sauces while grilling over coals. Most marinades can be used to baste meat, but remember that those containing high sugar levels, such as jam, chutney and honey, tend to burn easily and could cause a bitter taste, and should be brushed over the meat towards the end of the cooking time.

Although brushes are usually used, sprigs of herbs, such as rosemary, used as a basting brush provide extra flavour.

FRUIT BASTE

125 ml (½ cup) apricot or any other fruit juice
15 ml (1 tbsp) fresh lemon juice
15 ml (1 tbsp) honey
2 ml (¼ tsp) grated lemon rind
5 ml (1 tsp) chopped fresh root ginger

1. Mix all ingredients together and baste meat, poultry or fish frequently during cooking.

Root ginger

ROSEMARY BASTE

125 ml (½ cup) olive oil
60 ml (¼ cup) fresh lemon juice or dry white wine
15 ml (1 tbsp) honey
2 cloves garlic, crushed
15 ml (1 tbsp) chopped fresh rosemary
or 5 ml (1 tsp) dried
salt and freshly ground black pepper to taste

1. Mix all ingredients together and use a sprig of rosemary to baste meat, poultry or fish frequently during cooking.

Variation
Substitute rosemary with any other herb of choice:
15 ml (1 tbsp) chopped fresh or 5 ml (1 tsp) dried

Rosemary

WINE BASTE
Use white wine for chicken and fish, and red for lamb and beef.

125 ml (½ cup) dry red or white wine
45 ml (3 tbsp) cooking oil
30 ml (2 tbsp) fresh lemon juice
2 ml (¼ tsp) soya sauce
2 ml (¼ tsp) Worcestershire sauce
1 clove garlic, crushed
salt and freshly ground black pepper to taste

1. Mix all ingredients together and baste frequently during cooking.

glazes

Glazes normally contain sugar-based ingredients such as fruit juice, honey or brown sugar as these give the meat a glossy, golden-brown colour. They can also form part of a baste.

Brush meat with glaze only during the last 10 minutes of cooking time to prevent burning.

HONEY GLAZE
This is an excellent glaze for lamb, pork or poultry.

30 ml (2 tbsp) honey
10 ml (2 tsp) soya sauce
30 ml (2 tbsp) tomato sauce
30 ml (2 tbsp) orange juice
30 ml (2 tbsp) brown vinegar
30 ml (2 tbsp) dry white wine
10 ml (2 tsp) mustard powder
2 cloves garlic, crushed
salt and freshly ground black pepper to taste

1. Mix all ingredients together.

Garlic

Mustard powder

BASIC QUICK GLAZES
PINEAPPLE
Can be used for lamb, pork or poultry.

125 ml (½ cup) pineapple juice
60 ml (¼ cup) honey
30 ml (2 tbsp) light brown sugar
5 ml (1 tsp) mustard powder

1. Mix all ingredients together.

APRICOT
Can be used for lamb, pork or poultry.

30 ml (2 tbsp) smooth apricot jam
30 ml (2 tbsp) fruit chutney
15 ml (1 tbsp) tomato sauce
30 ml (2 tbsp) wine vinegar
30 ml (2 tbsp) meat stock

1. Mix all ingredients together.

Rubs
Rubbing herbs and spices into food prior to grilling adds flavour, especially to fatty cuts of meat. Rubs contain no oils to moisten or acids to tenderize.

---

marinades

snacks

FRUIT KEBABS WITH PINEAPPLE DRESSING

Serve these tropical kebabs chilled as a light snack.

MAKES ABOUT 18

4 bananas
1 avocado
60 ml (¼ cup) fresh lemon juice
440 g can pineapple pieces, syrup reserved
125 g glacé cherries

PINEAPPLE DRESSING

30 ml (2 tbsp) cornflour
250 ml (1 cup) water
250 ml (1 cup) sugar
2 egg yolks
200 ml (¾ cup) reserved pineapple syrup
30 ml (2 tbsp) fresh lemon juice

1. Peel and cut bananas and avocado into 1.5 cm thick pieces. Sprinkle with lemon juice.
2. Thread fruit pieces, including pineapple and cherries, alternately onto wooden skewers.
3. For dressing: Mix cornflour, water, sugar and egg yolks in a heavy-based saucepan. Bring to the boil, whisking continuously.
4. Add half the pineapple syrup and stir constantly for about 1 minute until the mixture thickens. Add remaining pineapple syrup and lemon juice, heat through, then remove from heat.
5. Chill and pour over kebabs.

Tip

To prevent avocados from discolouring, pour boiling water over unpeeled avocados and leave to stand for about 1 minute before peeling. Alternatively, brush the flesh with lemon juice to prevent discolouring after removing skins.

CHICKEN LIVER PÂTÉ

250 g chicken livers
30 ml (2 tbsp) butter
125 g bacon, chopped
1 small onion, chopped
1 clove garlic, crushed
salt and freshly ground black pepper to taste
60 ml (¼ cup) fresh cream
30 ml (2 tbsp) medium cream sherry
2 ml (¼ tsp) grated nutmeg
10 ml (2 tsp) chopped fresh thyme or 3 ml (½ tsp) dried
olives, bay leaves or parsley to decorate

GLAZE

5 ml (1 tsp) gelatine
60 ml (¼ cup) chicken stock

1. Trim and wash the chicken livers, then cut them into small pieces.
2. Melt half the butter in a heavy-based saucepan and add chicken livers, bacon, onion and garlic and fry for a few minutes until the livers change colour. They should be cooked, but not brown.
3. Transfer to a food processor or liquidizer. Add the remaining ingredients, including remaining butter, and process to a smooth consistency.
4. Transfer to serving dish, cover and refrigerate for at least 1 hour.
5. For glaze: Heat gelatine and chicken stock in the microwave for 30 seconds on 100% power or dissolve over hot water.
6. Decorate pâté with olives, bay leaves or parsley and pour over glaze. Refrigerate for about 6 hours to set.

RIGHT: *Fruit Kebabs with Pineapple Dressing, Chipolatas with Mayonnaise Chutney (see page 28).*

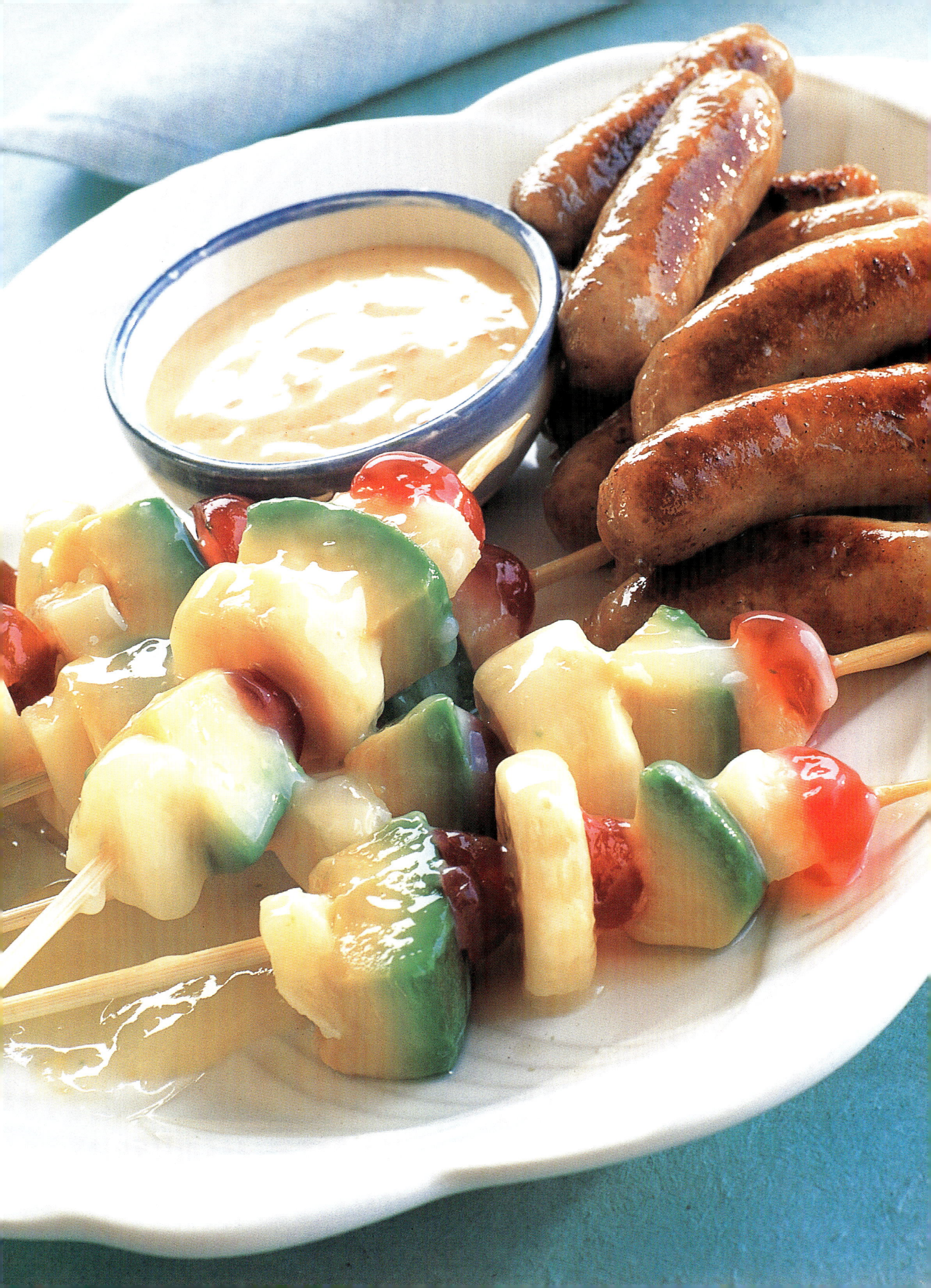

CHUTNEY CHEESY ROLLS

A delicious sweet and savoury combination.

MAKES ABOUT 15

200 g puff pastry (½ frozen packet), thawed
1 egg, beaten

FILLING

80 ml (⅓ cup) fruit chutney
75 g (¾ cup) grated Cheddar cheese

1. Preheat oven to 200 °C (400 °F).
2. Roll out pastry slightly into a 20 x 25 cm rectangular shape.
3. For filling: Mix all ingredients together and spread over entire surface of pastry. Roll up lengthwise as tightly as possible.
4. Cut pastry roll into 1 cm slices and place on a greased baking tray. Brush with beaten egg.
5. Bake for 10–12 minutes, then serve.

PERI-PERI PRAWNS

SERVES 4–6

30 (about 350 g) uncooked prawns
125 ml (½ cup) fresh lemon juice
100 g butter
4 cloves garlic, crushed
5 ml (1 tsp) hot peri-peri sauce
lemon wedges

1. Devein prawns. Marinate in 60 ml (¼ cup) lemon juice for about 30 minutes. Remove prawns and discard juice.
2. Heat a cast-iron plate or a skottel. Melt butter, add prawns with remaining lemon juice, garlic and peri-peri sauce.
3. Cook over moderate heat for 10–15 minutes, turning frequently in the sauce. Serve warm with lemon wedges.

FROM LEFT TO RIGHT: *Chutney Cheesy Rolls, Peri-peri Prawns.*

SMOKED SNOEK PÂTÉ

500 g smoked snoek, cut into chunks
250 g container smooth cottage cheese
80 ml (⅓ cup) fresh cream or milk
1 onion, finely chopped
15 ml (1 tbsp) fresh lemon juice
15 ml (1 tbsp) chopped fresh parsley
or 5 ml (1 tsp) dried
2 ml (¼ tsp) cayenne pepper
salt and freshly ground black pepper to taste

1. Mix the snoek with cottage cheese and cream.
2. Add remaining ingredients and mix until well combined.
3. Spoon into a serving dish and place in the refrigerator. Serve with Melba toast.

Melba toast
Cut bread into very thin slices and remove the crusts. Cut into triangular shapes and place in warm oven (150 °C/300° F) to dry out. Toast will curl up – allow to cool before serving.

SAVOURY CHEESE SLICES

MAKES 24

200 g (2 cups) grated Cheddar cheese
5 ml (1 tsp) mustard powder
15 ml (1 tbsp) Worcestershire sauce
2 eggs, beaten
2 ml (¼ tsp) salt
8 slices brown or white bread, 10 mm thick
125 g rindless streaky bacon

1. Mix cheese, mustard powder, Worcestershire sauce, eggs and salt. Spread on slices of bread.
2. Place 3 strips of bacon on top of the cheese mixture. Grill bread in the oven until bacon starts to brown.
3. Cut each slice into 3 strips and serve warm.

CREAMY AVOCADO DIP

SERVES 6–8

2 medium-sized ripe avocados
250 g container smooth cottage cheese
125 ml (½ cup) mayonnaise
45 ml (3 tbsp) fresh lemon juice
2 ml (¼ tsp) salt
2 ml (¼ tsp) mustard powder
3 drops Tabasco sauce

1. Combine all ingredients and mix until smooth.
2. Serve with bread or vegetable sticks.

TUNA DIP

*Delicious served with raw vegetable pieces
(such as carrots, celery, cucumber).*

SERVES 6–8

170 g can tuna chunks, drained
250 g container smooth cottage cheese or cream cheese
15 ml (1 tbsp) finely grated onion
2 ml (¼ tsp) Worcestershire sauce
5 ml (1 tsp) fresh lemon juice
3 drops Tabasco sauce
pinch of ground paprika
salt and freshly ground black pepper to taste

1. Combine all ingredients and mix together well.
2. Serve with Melba toast or health bread.

Variation
PINEAPPLE DIP
Substitute tuna with half a 440 g can crushed pineapple. Omit the Tabasco sauce, Worcestershire sauce and grated onion.

SPICY MEATBALLS WRAPPED IN BACON

MAKES ABOUT 12 KEBABS

15 ml (1 tbsp) olive oil
1 onion, chopped
1 clove garlic, crushed
500 g lean beef mince
250 ml (1 cup) freshly prepared brown
or white breadcrumbs
1 green apple, peeled and grated
5 ml (1 tsp) ground paprika
5 ml (1 tsp) chopped fresh thyme or 2 ml (¼ tsp) dried
salt and freshly ground black pepper to taste
125 g rindless streaky bacon

1. Heat the oil in a heavy-based saucepan and sauté the onion and garlic until soft. Remove from heat.
2. Mix with all other ingredients, except the bacon.
3. Roll meatballs by hand to about 35 mm in size. Wrap a bacon strip around each one and place in the refrigerator for about 1 hour to firm slightly.
4. Thread two meatballs per skewer, piercing through the bacon on each side.
5. Grill over moderate coals for 15–20 minutes until golden-brown.

Variation
DATE AND ALMOND KOFTAS
Omit breadcrumbs, apple and bacon. Add 250 g chopped dates and 100 g chopped almonds to mince mixture.

BACON-WRAPPED BANANAS

MAKES ABOUT 24

4 bananas, peeled
250 g rindless streaky bacon

1. Cut each banana into 6 pieces.
2. Cut bacon strips in half and wrap around each piece of banana. Secure with a toothpick.
3. Grill over moderate coals for about 10 minutes until golden-brown.

CHIPOLATAS WITH MAYONNAISE CHUTNEY

SERVES 4–6

500 g (about 18) chipolata sausages
125 ml (½ cup) mayonnaise
30 ml (2 tbsp) fruit chutney

1. Grill chipolata sausages over moderate coals for 10–15 minutes until cooked.
2. Mix mayonnaise and chutney and drizzle over hot chipolatas. Serve immediately.

Variation
Thread chipolatas onto skewers with lamb liver or chicken livers.

BARBECUED CHICKEN WINGS
Great as an appetizer to any meal.

SERVES 4–6

12 chicken wings
MARINADE
60 ml (¼ cup) olive oil
60 ml (¼ cup) soya sauce
60 ml (¼ cup) fruit chutney
60 ml (¼ cup) chilli sauce
60 ml (¼ cup) light brown sugar
30 ml (2 tbsp) fresh lemon juice
salt and freshly ground black pepper to taste

1. Cut off wing tips and scrape meat from the short bone towards the joint. This will act as a handle to hold onto when eating.
2. For marinade: Mix all ingredients together and pour over wings. Cover and leave to marinate in the refrigerator for 4–6 hours, or overnight if preferred.
3. Remove wings from marinade and grill over moderate coals for 12–15 minutes until golden-brown. Turn and baste frequently with marinade.

CLOCKWISE FROM LEFT: *Barbecued Chicken Wings, Spicy Meatballs wrapped in Bacon, Bacon-wrapped Bananas (see page 28).*

snacks 29

FROM TOP TO BOTTOM: *Bacon Pastry Twists, Chicken Satays with Peanut Sauce (see page 31).*

30 on the coals

BACON PASTRY TWISTS

MAKES ABOUT 30

200 g puff pastry (½ frozen packet), thawed
2 ml (¼ tsp) cayenne pepper
125 g rindless streaky bacon
1 egg, beaten

1. Preheat oven to 200 °C (400 °F).
2. Roll out pastry slightly, sprinkle with cayenne pepper and roll out further into a rectangular shape, about 20 x 25 cm.
3. Cut pastry into strips, 12 mm wide and 8 cm long.
4. Cut bacon strips in half lengthwise and cut to the length of the pastry strips.
5. Twist each pastry strip with a bacon strip. Place on a greased baking tray and press down the ends. Brush with beaten egg.
6. Bake for 10–12 minutes. Serve immediately.

ASPARAGUS AND POTATO CHIP CRISP

SERVES 4–6

440 g can asparagus salad cuts, water reserved
30 ml (2 tbsp) butter
30 ml (2 tbsp) cake flour
160 ml (⅔ cup) milk or cream
50 g (2 small packets) salt and vinegar chips
100 g (1 cup) grated Cheddar cheese
15 ml (1 tbsp) chopped fresh parsley or 5 ml (1 tsp) dried
2 ml (¼ tsp) cayenne pepper

1. Preheat oven to 200 °C (400 °F).
2. Melt butter in a heavy-based saucepan. Add flour and stir for about 2 minutes until flour is absorbed. Add milk or cream and 125 ml (½ cup) asparagus water, stirring constantly until the mixture thickens.
3. Add asparagus. Remove from heat and add crushed chips and grated cheese.
4. Spoon into individual serving dishes and sprinkle with parsley and cayenne pepper.
5. Bake for 10 minutes.

CHICKEN SATAYS WITH PEANUT SAUCE

MAKES ABOUT 14

4 deboned, skinned chicken breasts
MARINADE
1 small onion, finely chopped
1 clove garlic, crushed
15 ml (1 tbsp) chopped fresh root ginger
30 ml (2 tbsp) dark soya sauce
30 ml (2 tbsp) dried, crushed chillies (or to taste)
15 ml (1 tbsp) light brown sugar
15 ml (1 tbsp) fresh lemon juice
15 ml (1 tbsp) olive oil
PEANUT SAUCE
200 ml (¾ cup) coconut milk
60 ml (¼ cup) crunchy peanut butter
15 ml (1 tbsp) fresh lemon juice
salt and freshly ground black pepper to taste

1. Cut chicken into thin strips about 7 cm long.
2. For marinade: Combine all the ingredients and mix well. Add chicken and turn until well coated. Cover and leave in the refrigerator for 2–3 hours, or overnight if preferred.
3. Remove chicken from the marinade and thread the pieces, concertina-style onto thin wooden skewers.
4. Braai the chicken satays over moderate coals for 8–10 minutes, turning and basting occasionally with the marinade until cooked through.
5. For sauce: Mix all ingredients in a heavy-based saucepan. Bring to the boil and simmer for 3 minutes. Season to taste and serve with the cooked satays.

Making coconut milk

Pour 500 ml (2 cups) boiling water over 100 g (1 cup) desiccated coconut and simmer over low heat for 10 minutes. Strain the milk through a piece of muslin cloth or sieve into a bowl. Makes about 300 ml.

meat

beef & veal

BEER MARINATED STEAKS

SERVES 4

4 blade or sirloin steaks, 25 mm thick
MARINADE
340 ml (1 can) beer
60 ml (¼ cup) olive oil
30 ml (2 tbsp) fresh lemon juice
2 ml (¼ tsp) grated lemon rind
1 bay leaf
15 ml (1 tbsp) light brown sugar
15 ml (1 tbsp) chopped fresh root ginger
salt and freshly ground black pepper to taste

1. Slash edges of fat at 25 mm intervals.
2. For marinade: Mix all ingredients together and pour over meat. Marinate in the refrigerator for 2–3 hours.
3. Remove steaks from marinade and pat dry with paper towel.
4. Braai over hot coals for 8–10 minutes for medium-done, turning and basting frequently with marinade. Serve immediately.

T-BONE WITH GREEN PEPPERCORN SAUCE

SERVES 2

2 T-bone steaks, 25 mm thick
SAUCE
30 ml (2 tbsp) butter
1 onion, finely chopped
1 clove garlic, crushed
45 ml (3 tbsp) green peppercorns, lightly crushed
80 ml (⅓ cup) milk
125 ml (½ cup) fresh cream
20 ml (4 tsp) brandy (optional)
5 ml (1 tsp) chopped fresh parsley or 2 ml (¼ tsp) dried
5 ml (1 tsp) salt

1. For sauce: Heat butter in a heavy-based saucepan, add the onion and garlic and sauté until soft.
2. Add peppercorns and stir for a few minutes.
3. Add all remaining sauce ingredients and stir frequently over medium heat for 20–30 minutes until thickened.
4. Braai steak over hot coals for about 10 minutes for medium-done. Serve immediately with the sauce.

Variation
Substitute green peppercorns with capers.

Green peppercorns
These peppercorns can be pickled in vinegar or brine. They have a hot pickle taste and are used to flavour meat, venison, duck, sausages and sauces. Use whole or coarsely crushed.

RIGHT: *T-bone with green peppercorn sauce.*

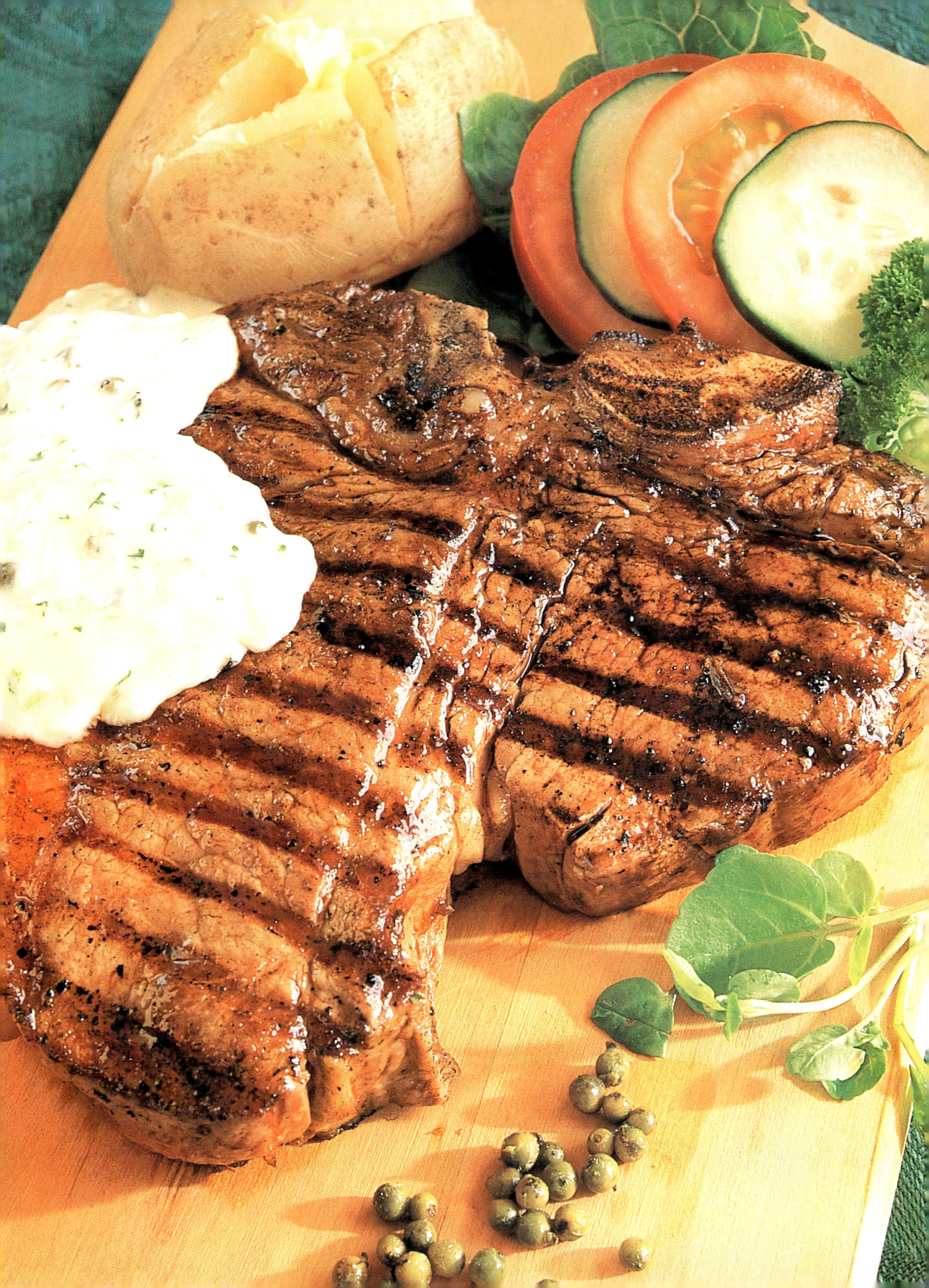

ABOVE: *Beef patties (burgers) (see page 35).*

BEEF PATTIES (BURGERS)

Always an economical and versatile way of entertaining when served with a choice of irresistible sauces.

MAKES ABOUT 12 LARGE

45 ml (3 tbsp) cooking oil
2 onions, chopped
2 cloves garlic, crushed
1 kg lean beef mince
250 ml (1 cup) freshly prepared brown
or white breadcrumbs
60 ml (¼ cup) chopped fresh parsley
or 20 ml (4 tsp) dried
salt and freshly ground black pepper to taste

1. Heat oil in a heavy-based saucepan and sauté onion and garlic until soft.
2. Transfer to a large mixing bowl and add all remaining ingredients. Divide the mixture into 12 patties, about 25 mm thick.
3. Brush grid lightly with oil. Braai patties over moderate coals for 10–12 minutes until cooked. A skottel can also be used for braaiing patties.
4. Serve with Creamy mushroom or Barbecue sauce.

Variation
For a curry flavour, add 10 ml (2 tsp) medium curry powder when frying the onion.

Tips
- Use a spatula or tongs when turning patties to maintain their shape.
- Avoid pressing down patties while grilling as this squeezes out the juices and dries the patties out.
- Never cook burgers to the point where they become dry, but make sure that they are cooked through, with no sign of any pink meat.

CREAMY MUSHROOM SAUCE

45 g butter
1 large onion, chopped
1 clove garlic, crushed
45 ml (3 tbsp) cake flour
250 g button mushrooms, sliced
250 ml (1 cup) milk
125 ml (½ cup) fresh cream
30 ml (2 tbsp) chopped fresh parsley
or 10 ml (2 tsp) dried
salt and freshly ground black pepper to taste
45 ml (3 tbsp) muscadel (optional)

1. Heat butter and sauté onion and garlic until soft.
2. Add flour, stirring for about 2 minutes.
3. Add remaining ingredients and simmer for about 15 minutes, stirring occasionally until thickened.

BARBECUE SAUCE

15 ml (1 tbsp) cooking oil
1 onion, finely chopped
2 cloves garlic, crushed
500 g (± 5) tomatoes, peeled and chopped
10 ml (2 tsp) tomato paste
30 ml (2 tbsp) light brown sugar
30 ml (2 tbsp) vinegar
15 ml (1 tbsp) Worcestershire sauce
salt and freshly ground black pepper to taste
5 ml (1 tsp) cake flour

1. Heat oil in a heavy-based saucepan and sauté onion and garlic for a few minutes until soft.
2. Add tomatoes and stir well.
3. Add all remaining ingredients, except flour, and simmer for about 20 minutes, stirring occasionally. To thicken, mix flour with a little water and stir into the sauce.

PESTO STEAKS

SERVES 4

4 fillet steaks, 30 mm thick
45 ml (3 tbsp) prepared pesto
salt and freshly ground black pepper to taste

1. Use a sharp knife to cut a horizontal slit in the centre of each steak, making a pocket for filling. Place about 10 ml (2 tsp) pesto sauce in each pocket and secure with toothpicks.
2. Braai over hot coals for 10–12 minutes for medium-done. Season with salt and pepper and serve immediately.

Almond pesto sauce

3 cloves garlic, finely crushed
80 g fresh basil leaves, chopped
125 ml (½ cup) olive oil
salt and freshly ground black pepper to taste
60 g finely grated Parmesan cheese
45 ml (3 tbsp) finely chopped almonds

Mix garlic and basil in a food processor until a paste is formed. Add olive oil gradually while blending again. Season with salt and pepper and add cheese and nuts to form a thick sauce. Spoon into a jar, top with a thin layer of oil and seal tightly. It will keep in the refrigerator for up to two weeks.

Pesto
The main ingredients in a pesto sauce are basil and Parmesan cheese. When basil is in season, make pesto and freeze it for later use. It can be kept for up to six months.

RUMP STEAK WITH LEMON-GARLIC BUTTER

SERVES 4

4 rump steaks, 25 mm thick
salt and freshly ground black pepper to taste
lemon-garlic butter (see page 93)

1. Slash edges of fat at 25 mm intervals.
2. Braai meat over hot coals for about 10 minutes for medium-done. Season and serve steak immediately with lemon-garlic, Italian or other savoury butters.

STEAK KEBABS WITH RED WINE BASTE

The red wine adds flavour and keeps the meat moist.

MAKES ABOUT 8

500 g rump steak, cut into 25 mm cubes
125 g rindless streaky bacon, cut into 20 mm long strips
12–15 pickling onions, halved
125 g button mushrooms, halved

BASTING SAUCE

125 ml (½ cup) dry red wine
30 ml (2 tbsp) tomato sauce
2 cloves garlic, crushed
5 ml (1 tsp) chopped fresh thyme or 2 ml (¼ tsp) dried
5 ml (1 tsp) medium chilli sauce
salt and freshly ground black pepper to taste

1. Thread the steak cubes onto skewers, alternating with bacon, onions and mushrooms.
2. For basting: Mix all ingredients together.
3. Braai kebabs over moderate coals for 15–20 minutes, turning and basting frequently until dark brown. Serve immediately.

Onions
If you find the pickling onions too hard, blanch them in boiling water for 1 minute to soften slightly.

FROM TOP TO BOTTOM: *Steak Kebabs with Red Wine Baste, Pesto Steaks (see page 36).*

meat 37

PEPPER-ORIGANUM STEAKS

SERVES 6

6 club or fillet steaks, 25 mm thick
30 ml (2 tbsp) olive oil
45 ml (3 tbsp) freshly ground black pepper
30 ml (2 tbsp) chopped fresh origanum
or 10 ml (2 tsp) dried
salt to taste

1. Slash edges of fat at 25 mm intervals. Brush steaks with olive oil.
2. Mix pepper, origanum and salt and roll each steak in the mixture to cover the entire surface.
3. Braai steak over hot coals for about 10 minutes for medium-done. Serve immediately.

CLOCKWISE FROM TOP: *Pasta Salad (see page 103), Pepper-Origanum Steaks, Veal in Sherry Sauce (see page 39).*

BOEREWORS (TRADITIONAL SAUSAGE)

*Making sausage is not as difficult as it seems.
Adjust spices to personal taste.*

MAKES ABOUT 5.5 KG

4 kg beef, cut into 25 mm cubes
2 kg pork, cut into 25 mm cubes
60 ml (¼ cup) whole coriander
60 ml (¼ cup) salt
10 ml (2 tsp) freshly ground black pepper
5 ml (1 tsp) grated nutmeg
2 ml (¼ tsp) ground cloves
250 ml (1 cup) vinegar
± 200 g pork or mutton casing

1. Layer all the meat in a large dish.
2. Sear the coriander in a heavy-based saucepan over medium heat. Leave to cool and grind well. Sift to remove husks.
3. Mix all dry ingredients and sprinkle over meat. Mix well.
4. Add vinegar and mix well. Spoon mixture into a sausage maker.
5. Fill casing and leave for at least 24 hours in the refrigerator to allow the flavours to develop. Can be frozen for up to two months.
6. Braai over moderate coals for about 20 minutes for well-done.

Casing
Before use, soak the casing in lukewarm water for 30 minutes and then rinse out with cold water to remove excess salt.

Pepper
Probably the most popular spice. Green, red, black and white peppercorns all come from the same pepper plant, the colour reflecting the state of maturity or type of processing. On drying, the peppercorns become black. Black peppercorns are hot and spicy to the palate, while green is fruitier and pungent. Pepper is at its most aromatic when freshly ground.

VEAL IN SHERRY SAUCE

SERVES 4

6 veal schnitzels, 3–5 mm thick
salt and freshly ground black pepper to taste
80 ml (⅓ cup) cake flour
20 ml (4 tsp) butter
30 ml (2 tbsp) olive oil
125 ml (½ cup) medium cream sherry
200 ml (¾ cup) chicken stock

1. Season schnitzels with salt and pepper. Coat with flour.
2. Melt butter and oil in a flat cast-iron pan over hot coals. Fry veal on both sides until golden-brown. Spoon off remaining butter and oil from pan and add sherry and chicken stock.
3. Cover and simmer for 10–15 minutes. If necessary, thicken sauce with flour mixed with water.

CONCERTINA VEAL KEBABS WITH LITCHI SAUCE

MAKES ABOUT 8

500 g veal steak
410 g can litchis, drained and liquid reserved

SAUCE
30 ml (2 tbsp) butter
30 ml (2 tbsp) cake flour
30 ml (2 tbsp) fresh cream
80 ml (⅓ cup) milk
20 ml (4 tsp) fresh lemon juice
salt and freshly ground black pepper to taste

1. Cut veal into strips measuring 10 x 50 mm.
2. Thread onto skewers, alternating with litchis.
3. For sauce: Heat butter in a heavy-based saucepan, add flour and stir for a few minutes. Add 125 ml (½ cup) reserved litchi juice and bring to the boil, stirring.
4. Add fresh cream, milk, lemon juice and seasoning. Simmer sauce for about 5 minutes.
5. Braai kebabs over moderate coals for 15–20 minutes. Serve with warm sauce.

CARPETBAG STEAKS

SERVES 4

4 rump steaks, 30 mm thick
FILLING
10 ml (2 tsp) butter
125 g button mushrooms, chopped
85 g can smoked oysters
15 ml (1 tbsp) fresh lemon juice
15 ml (1 tbsp) medium cream sherry
15 ml (1 tbsp) chopped fresh parsley or 5 ml (1 tsp) dried
salt and freshly ground black pepper to taste

1. Slash edges of fat at 25 mm intervals.
2. Use a sharp knife to cut a horizontal slit in the thick centre of each steak to make a pocket for filling.
3. For filling: Melt butter and fry mushrooms lightly. Remove from heat and add remaining ingredients. Fill pockets and secure with toothpicks.
4. Braai steaks over hot coals for 18–20 minutes for medium-done. Remove toothpicks, season and serve immediately.

FILLET WITH CHILLI SAUCE

SERVES 4–6

6 fillet steaks, 25 mm thick
CHILLI SAUCE
125 ml (½ cup) medium chilli sauce
30 ml (2 tbsp) olive oil
2 ml (¼ tsp) Worcestershire sauce
2 ml (¼ tsp) soya sauce
15 ml (1 tbsp) spirit or grape vinegar
2 cloves garlic, crushed
2 ml (¼ tsp) medium curry powder
30 ml (2 tbsp) fresh lemon juice
salt and freshly ground black pepper to taste

1. For sauce: Mix all ingredients in a heavy-based saucepan. Bring to the boil and simmer for about 5 minutes.
2. Braai fillet over hot coals for 8–10 minutes for medium-done. Serve immediately with sauce.

SHORT RIB WITH COLA

SERVES 6

800 g short rib, cut into 40 mm portions
MARINADE
15 ml (1 tbsp) butter
1 onion, finely chopped
200 ml (¾ cup) cola
80 ml (⅓ cup) tomato sauce
45 ml (3 tbsp) fresh lemon juice
10 ml (2 tsp) chilli sauce
salt and freshly ground black pepper to taste

1. For marinade: Heat butter in a heavy-based saucepan. Sauté onion until soft. Add all remaining ingredients and simmer for 10 minutes. Leave to cool.
2. Pour over meat and marinate in refrigerator for 4–6 hours, or overnight if preferred.
3. Remove meat from marinade. Braai over moderate coals for about 30 minutes until golden-brown, turning and basting frequently with marinade. Serve immediately.

SALT-CRUST ROAST IN COALS

SERVES 6–8

2 kg topside
10 ml (2 tsp) freshly ground black pepper
± 1 kg fine table salt
± 5 kg charcoal

1. Make a large, compact fire using only charcoal.
2. Cover topside completely with pepper and as much salt as possible.
3. Make a hole in the centre of red-hot coals, leaving a layer for the meat to be placed upon.
4. Carefully place the meat in the centre of the coals and cover all round with coals. Cook for 70 minutes (1.5 kg takes 55 minutes) for rare to medium-done.
5. Gently remove coals and take out the meat. Shake off most of the salt, then cut the meat into thin slices.
6. Serve immediately with Creamy mushroom sauce or Barbecue sauce (see page 35).

Salt-crust Roast (see page 40) with Barbecue Sauce (see page 35).

PORTERHOUSE STEAK WITH MUSTARD-SHERRY SAUCE

SERVES 2

1 porterhouse steak, 50 mm thick

SAUCE

20 ml (4 tsp) butter
2 spring onions, chopped
200 ml (¾ cup) fresh cream
30 ml (2 tbsp) muscadel or sherry
10 ml (2 tsp) chopped fresh parsley or
3 ml (½ tsp) dried
5 ml (1 tsp) chopped fresh thyme or 2 ml (¼ tsp) dried
10 ml (2 tsp) prepared mustard
salt and freshly ground black pepper to taste

1. For sauce: Heat butter in a heavy-based saucepan, add onions and sauté until soft. Add remaining sauce ingredients and stir over medium heat for 20–30 minutes until thickened.
2. Braai meat over hot coals for about 18 minutes for medium-done. Serve immediately with the sauce.

Tip
For a healthier option, omit the cream and add 200 ml (¾ cup) plain, unflavoured yoghurt when the sauce is cooked.

meat 41

mutton & lamb

CUTLETS WITH ROASTED RED PEPPER SAUCE

SERVES 8

8 lamb cutlets, 20 mm thick
SAUCE
2 large red peppers, seeded and quartered
250 ml (1 cup) vegetable stock
30 ml (2 tbsp) butter
30 ml (2 tbsp) cake flour
10 ml (2 tsp) chopped fresh mixed herbs
or 3 ml (½ tsp) dried
salt and freshly ground black pepper to taste
45 ml (3 tbsp) fresh cream

1. Roast peppers on a baking tray in the oven at 200 °C (400 °F) for about 15 minutes, or use char-grilled vegetables (see page 96). Skin peppers, chop roughly and blend with stock to make a thin purée.
2. Melt butter in a heavy-based saucepan, add flour and stir for a few minutes. Add the pepper purée, herbs and seasoning. Bring to the boil.
3. Whisk to ensure a smooth consistency and simmer for about 5 minutes. Add cream.
4. Braai cutlets over moderate coals for 15–20 minutes until done. Serve with warm sauce.

Tip
To peel the skins off grilled peppers, pop into a plastic bag while still hot and set aside for about 10 minutes. The steam will help to remove the skins.

Cutlets
These are rib chops where the back-bone has been removed (chined) and the tips of the rib bones have been cut away (frenched).

GINGER-FLAVOURED KEBABS
Kebabs originate from Turkey, where lamb is traditionally threaded onto metal skewers with a variety of fruit or vegetables.

MAKES ABOUT 8

500 g leg of lamb, cut into 25 mm cubes
8 pickling onions, cut in half
1 pineapple, peeled and cut into wedges
2 green peppers, seeded and cut into squares
MARINADE
30 ml (2 tbsp) finely chopped fresh root ginger
3 ml (½ tsp) cayenne pepper
30 ml (2 tbsp) red wine vinegar
45 ml (3 tbsp) fresh lemon juice
salt and freshly ground black pepper to taste

1. For marinade: Mix all ingredients together and pour over meat. Cover and marinate in the refrigerator for 2–3 hours, turning occasionally.
2. Thread meat onto skewers, alternating with onions, pineapple and green pepper.
3. Braai over moderate coals for about 20 minutes until done, turning and basting frequently with marinade. Serve immediately.

Ginger
Root ginger is found in many forms: fresh, powdered or dried. Powdered or dried ginger lasts longer than fresh, which if stored in a cool dry place should last at least two months. It is used in drinks such as ginger ale, and in cakes as well as preserves. It is also a basic ingredient in curries.

42 on the coals

FROM TOP TO BOTTOM: *Ginger-flavoured Kebabs, Cutlets with Roasted Red Pepper Sauce (see page 42).*

meat 43

SPIRAL SAUSAGE ON A SKEWER
An interesting way of serving familiar sausage!

SERVES 4–6

1 kg lamb sausage

1. Divide sausage into about 4–6 sections.
2. Roll each firmly on a skewer, in a spiral form.
3. Braai over moderate-low coals for 15–20 minutes, depending on thickness of sausage, until done.
4. Serve with Barbecue sauce (see page 35).

LAMB WITH LEMON AND MINT

SERVES 4–6

6 lamb loin chops, 20 mm thick
MARINADE
80 ml (⅓ cup) fresh lemon juice
5 ml (1 tsp) grated lemon rind
15 ml (1 tbsp) chopped fresh mint or 5 ml (1 tsp) dried
45 ml (3 tbsp) port or sherry (optional)

1. For marinade: Mix all ingredients together. Pour over meat and marinade for 30 minutes.
2. Braai chops over moderate coals for 15–20 minutes, turning and basting frequently with the marinade until done.

CLOCKWISE FROM TOP: *Traditional Sosaties (see page 45), Spiral Sausage on a Skewer, Barbecue Chops (see page 45).*

BARBECUE CHOPS

This barbecue sauce can be used for any other meat or poultry.

SERVES 4–6

6 lamb noisettes, 20 mm thick
MARINADE
30 ml (2 tbsp) butter
1 medium onion, chopped
2 cloves garlic, crushed
45 ml (3 tbsp) light brown sugar
60 ml (¼ cup) vinegar
5 ml (1 tsp) mustard powder
125 ml (½ cup) tomato sauce
125 ml (½ cup) water
15 ml (1 tbsp) Worcestershire sauce
15 ml (1 tbsp) fresh lemon juice
salt and freshly ground black pepper to taste

1. For marinade: Heat butter in a heavy-based saucepan and sauté onion and garlic until soft. Add all remaining ingredients and simmer for about 20 minutes. Leave to cool.
2. Pour over meat and marinate in the refrigerator for 2–3 hours.
3. Braai chops over moderate coals for 15–20 minutes, turning and basting frequently with marinade until cooked and golden-brown.

Variation

For a coffee flavour, add 60 ml (¼ cup) strong coffee to the marinade when simmering in saucepan.

Noisettes

These are deboned ribs, rolled and cut at 25 mm intervals. Secure with string or thread onto a skewer.

TRADITIONAL SOSATIES

Made from cubed lamb, spek (fat) and dried apricots threaded onto skewers, then covered with a curry marinade.

MAKES ABOUT 15

1 kg deboned leg of lamb or mutton,
cut into 25 mm squares
200 g spek, cut into 10 mm squares
125 g dried apricots
CURRY MARINADE
15 ml (1 tbsp) cooking oil
3 onions, sliced
20 ml (4 tsp) medium curry powder
2 ml (¼ tsp) turmeric
2 ml (¼ tsp) ground ginger
10 ml (2 tsp) chilli sauce (optional)
30 ml (2 tbsp) smooth apricot jam
30 ml (2 tbsp) light brown sugar
2 bay leaves or lemon leaves
625 ml (2½ cups) vinegar
125 ml (½ cup) milk
salt and freshly ground black pepper to taste
15 ml (1 tbsp) cake flour

1. For marinade: Heat cooking oil in a heavy-based saucepan and sauté onions until soft. Add curry powder and turmeric and fry lightly.
2. Add remaining ingredients. (When adding milk, the mixture will have a curdled appearance.) Simmer for 10 minutes, then leave to cool slightly.
3. Thread pieces of lamb, spek and apricots onto skewers. Pour marinade over the sosaties, cover and place in the refrigerator for 1–2 days, turning occasionally.
4. Braai sosaties over moderate coals for 20–25 minutes, turning and basting frequently with marinade until cooked and golden-brown.

Turmeric

Belongs to the same family as ginger. The root is dried and then finely ground to produce a bright yellow powder that adds colour and flavour to foods such as mustard, chutney and curries. If kept too long, the flavour will deteriorate.

TANDOORI MUTTON CHOPS

Although chicken is most often used for this Indian-style recipe, this version uses lamb chops, coated in yoghurt and spices.

SERVES 4–6

6 mutton chump chops, 20 mm thick
MARINADE
350 ml (2 x 175 g tubs) plain low-fat yoghurt
10 ml (2 tsp) ground cumin
15 ml (1 tbsp) ground coriander
10 ml (2 tsp) medium curry powder
3 cloves garlic, crushed
10 ml (2 tsp) chopped fresh mint or 3 ml (½ tsp) dried
15 ml (1 tbsp) fresh lemon juice

1. For marinade: Mix all ingredients together and pour over meat.
2. Cover and marinate in the refrigerator for 4–6 hours, or overnight if preferred.
3. Remove lamb from marinade and braai over moderate coals for 15–20 minutes until done. Serve immediately.

Cumin
These small, dark brown seeds are available whole or ground. They are an essential ingredient in curry powder, and are frequently used in Indian and Middle Eastern dishes. The whole seeds are strong with a spicy, bitter taste and are sometimes used in pickling. Cumin is not suitable for sweet dishes.

Tip
This dish can also be prepared on a skottel or cast-iron plate.

CORIANDER LAMB RIB

SERVES 4–6

1 kg lamb rib
30 ml (2 tbsp) whole coriander
5 ml (1 tsp) barbecue spice
15 ml (1 tbsp) chopped fresh rosemary
or 5 ml (1 tsp) dried
salt and freshly ground black pepper to taste

1. Sear coriander in a heavy-based saucepan over medium heat. Cool, then grind well. Sift to remove husks.
2. Mix coriander, barbecue spice, rosemary and seasoning and rub over rib.
3. Braai over moderate coals for about 20 minutes, or until done.

Coriander
These brown seeds have a slightly spicy, orange flavour. They can be used whole in pickles, or crushed and ground for lentil dishes, curries and sausages.

LAMB WITH CARAMELIZED ONIONS

SERVES 4–6

6 lamb loin chops, 20 mm thick
50 g butter
200 g onions, peeled and quartered
15 ml (1 tbsp) light brown sugar
10 ml (2 tsp) red or white wine vinegar
salt and freshly ground black pepper to taste

1. Melt butter in a heavy-based saucepan, add onions and fry lightly for about 10 minutes until softened, but not browned.
2. Add sugar, vinegar and seasoning and continue to simmer for another 5 minutes.
3. Braai chops over moderate coals for 15–20 minutes until done. Serve with onions.

FROM LEFT TO RIGHT: *Tandoori Mutton Chops (see page 46), Glazed Lamb Riblets.*

GLAZED LAMB RIBLETS

Delicious as a pre-braai nibble.

SERVES 4–6

10 lamb riblets (± 650 g)

GLAZE

30 ml (2 tbsp) honey

10 ml (2 tsp) soya sauce

30 ml (2 tbsp) tomato sauce

30 ml (2 tbsp) orange juice

30 ml (2 tbsp) brown spirit vinegar

30 ml (2 tbsp) dry white wine

3 cloves garlic, crushed

10 ml (2 tsp) mustard powder

salt and freshly ground black pepper to taste

1. For glaze: Mix all ingredients together.
2. Braai over hot coals for 15–20 minutes until cooked and golden-brown, turning and basting frequently with the glaze.

Variation

The glaze is also excellent with pork. Baste 6 pork chops with glaze and braai for about 25 minutes.

meat 47

CITRUS LAMB

SERVES 4–6

6 chump chops, 20 mm thick
MARINADE
125 ml (½ cup) orange juice
10 ml (2 tsp) grated orange rind
30 ml (2 tbsp) olive oil
15 ml (1 tbsp) Worcestershire sauce
15 ml (1 tbsp) light brown sugar
15 ml (1 tbsp) chopped fresh mixed herbs
or 5 ml (1 tsp) dried
salt and freshly ground black pepper to taste

1. For marinade: Mix all ingredients together. Pour over meat and marinate in refrigerator for 30 minutes.
2. Braai chops over moderate coals for about 15 minutes, turning and basting frequently with marinade until done.

Tip
When grating orange and lemon rind, only grate the rind and not the white pith, which gives a bitter flavour to the dish.

LAMB SHOULDER BLADE WITH ROSEMARY BASTE

SERVES 4–6

1 lamb shoulder blade (± 1.2 kg), deboned
3 cloves garlic, peeled and thinly sliced
1 sprig rosemary, divided in small pieces
1 large sprig rosemary for basting
ROSEMARY BASTE (see page 22)

1. Cut incisions in skin of lamb and place garlic slices and a small sprig of rosemary in each.
2. Braai over moderate coals for about 1 hour for medium-done. Use the large sprig of rosemary to baste the meat frequently with the basting sauce. Serve immediately.

Rosemary
This dull green, bushy shrub with needle-shaped leaves has a strong, pungent flavour and should be used sparingly. Rosemary is best used on its own to flavour lamb, pork and poultry as it can overpower other herbs.

STIR-FRY WITH PASTA
Any left-over vegetables can be used for this dish.

SERVES 4

60 g uncooked pasta shells or linguine
400 g lamb, cut from leg or shoulder
30 ml (2 tbsp) cooking oil
1 clove garlic, crushed
2 leeks, sliced
50 g cabbage, shredded
125 g button mushrooms, sliced
1 red or green pepper, seeded and sliced
salt and freshly ground black pepper to taste
SAUCE
60 ml (¼ cup) medium cream sherry
20 ml (4 tsp) sugar
30 ml (2 tbsp) soya sauce
20 ml (4 tsp) fresh lemon juice
5 ml (1 tsp) sesame seeds
5 ml (1 tsp) cornflour

1. Cook pasta until soft. Rinse under cold water to prevent it sticking together and set aside.
2. Cut lamb into 8 x 40 mm strips.
3. Heat oil on a cast-iron plate or on a skottel and fry lamb until golden-brown.
4. Add garlic and leeks and sauté until soft. Add cabbage, mushrooms, pepper and seasoning.
5. For sauce: Mix all ingredients together and pour over meat. Add pasta and stir-fry for a few minutes. Serve immediately.

ORIENTAL LEG OF LAMB

SERVES 4–6

1 leg of lamb (± 1.8 kg), butterflied
MARINADE
250 ml (1 cup) buttermilk
30 ml (2 tbsp) olive oil
15 ml (1 tbsp) finely chopped root ginger
10 ml (2 tsp) medium curry powder
10 ml (2 tsp) ground cumin
30 ml (2 tbsp) fruit chutney
15 ml (1 tbsp) tomato paste
4 cloves garlic, crushed
salt and freshly ground black pepper to taste

1. For marinade: Mix all ingredients together. Pour over meat, cover and marinate in the refrigerator for 6–8 hours, or overnight if preferred.
2. Braai over moderate-low coals for about 1 hour for medium-done, turning and basting occasionally with marinade. Serve immediately.

MUTTON CHOPS WITH TOMATO AND THYME

SERVES 4–6

6 mutton rib chops, 20 mm thick
MARINADE
60 ml (¼ cup) olive oil
60 ml (¼ cup) tomato sauce
30 ml (2 tbsp) Worcestershire sauce
30 ml (2 tbsp) fresh lemon juice
30 ml (2 tbsp) soft brown sugar
15 ml (1 tbsp) chopped fresh thyme or 5 ml (1 tsp) dried
salt and freshly ground black pepper to taste

1. For marinade: Mix all ingredients together and pour over meat. Cover and marinate in the refrigerator for 30 minutes.
2. Remove chops from marinade and braai over moderate coals for about 15 minutes until cooked and golden-brown, turning and basting frequently with marinade. Serve immediately.

Thyme
This low-growing herb with its dull green leaves is a favourite to use in bouquet garni, soups and sauces, and goes with all meat. It dries well.

HONEY AND CHUTNEY CHOPS

Chutney is a simple, easy glaze – the honey adds a delicate sweetness.

SERVES 4–6

8 lamb loin chops, 20 mm thick
BASTING SAUCE
80 ml (⅓ cup) fruit chutney
45 ml (3 tbsp) honey
10 ml (2 tsp) chopped fresh parsley or 3 ml (½ tsp) dried
5 ml (1 tsp) finely chopped fresh rosemary or 2 ml (¼ tsp) dried
5 ml (1 tsp) mustard powder
2 ml (¼ tsp) medium curry powder
salt and freshly ground black pepper to taste

1. For basting sauce: Mix all ingredients together.
2. Braai chops over moderate coals for 15–20 minutes until cooked and golden-brown, turning and basting frequently with sauce towards the end of the cooking time. Serve immediately.

Parsley
This is the most frequently used herb. It is a plant with bright green leaves, which are either curled or flat, and is rich in Vitamins A, B and C. Providing colour and interest to most foods, it can be finely chopped and sprinkled over dishes before serving, or added to sauces. It is handy to keep some pre-chopped parsley in the refrigerator.

pork

BARBECUE SPARE RIBS

SERVES 4–6

1 kg pork spare ribs
MARINADE
60 ml (¼ cup) olive oil
30 ml (2 tbsp) soya sauce
30 ml (2 tbsp) honey
10 ml (2 tsp) prepared mustard
30 ml (2 tbsp) tomato sauce
30 ml (2 tbsp) smooth apricot jam
4 cloves garlic, crushed
salt and freshly ground black pepper to taste

1. For marinade: Mix all ingredients together and pour over ribs.
2. Cover and marinate in the refrigerator for 4–6 hours, or overnight if preferred.
3. Braai ribs over moderate coals for 15–20 minutes until golden-brown, basting frequently with marinade. Cut into portions.
4. Warm remaining marinade and serve immediately with ribs.

Soya sauce
Both light and dark sauces are available. Light soya sauce is thinner and normally used with poultry and vegetable dishes where the colours and flavours of the ingredients should not be overpowered. Dark soya sauce complements beef and other dark meat dishes. It can be used in marinades, stir-fries and soups.

PORK RASHERS WITH GARLIC AND ROSEMARY BASTE

These grill quickly and are ideal as a starter.

SERVES 4

6 pork rashers (± 550 g), 20 mm thick
BASTING SAUCE
80 ml (⅓ cup) dry white wine
45 ml (3 tbsp) fresh lemon juice
5 ml (1 tsp) grated lemon rind
45 ml (3 tbsp) olive oil
2 cloves garlic, crushed
15 ml (1 tbsp) chopped fresh rosemary
or 5 ml (1 tsp) dried
salt and freshly ground black pepper to taste

1. For basting sauce: Mix all ingredients together.
2. Braai rashers over moderate coals for 20–25 minutes, turning and basting them frequently until golden-brown. Use a sprig of rosemary to apply the baste.

Garlic
This has become an essential cooking ingredient. Cooking garlic more slowly and for longer, will sweeten the flavour and reduce the strong smell. The flavour of fresh garlic is superior to dried or ready-chopped in jars. Store fresh garlic in a cool, dry place for a few weeks.

PORK FILLET FOR SALAD

A distinct and marvellous flavour. Superb for salads.

600 g pork fillet
MARINADE
30 ml (2 tbsp) soya sauce
45 ml (3 tbsp) medium cream sherry
2 cloves garlic, crushed
30 ml (2 tbsp) coarsely chopped root ginger
15 ml (1 tbsp) olive oil

1. For marinade: Mix all ingredients together and pour over meat. Cover and marinate in the refrigerator for 2–3 hours, turning occasionally.
2. Braai fillet over moderate coals for about 20 minutes, turning and basting frequently with the marinade until done.
3. Cut into 20 mm thick slices and use in a salad.

GAMMON STEAKS WITH APRICOT GLAZE

SERVES 6

6 gammon steaks, 15 mm thick
GLAZE
30 ml (2 tbsp) smooth apricot jam
15 ml (1 tbsp) fruit chutney
5 ml (1 tsp) tomato sauce
30 ml (2 tbsp) fresh lemon juice

1. For glaze: Mix all ingredients together.
2. Braai steaks over moderate coals for 8–10 minutes, turning and basting frequently with the glaze until done.

Variation
Use 125 ml (½ cup) marmalade for glazing.

CLOCKWISE FROM TOP: *Broccoli Salad (see page 103), Pork Rashers with Garlic and Rosemary Baste (see page 50), Barbecue Spare Ribs (see page 50).*

Pork Roast (see page 53).

52 on the coals

DRIED FRUIT STUFFED PORK CHOPS

SERVES 8

8 pork loin chops, 30 mm thick
FILLING
100 g (¾ cup) chopped dried apricots
100 g (¾ cup) slightly chopped raisins
125 ml (½ cup) freshly prepared brown
or white breadcrumbs
10 ml (2 tsp) fresh lemon juice
15 ml (1 tbsp) butter, melted
15 ml (1 tbsp) chopped fresh parsley
or 5 ml (1 tsp) dried
salt and freshly ground black pepper to taste

1. Trim excess fat from chops, then slash the edges of the remaining fat at 25 mm intervals.
2. Use a sharp knife to cut a horizontal slit in the thick section of each chop to make a pocket for the filling.
3. For filling: Mix all ingredients together, then place about 30 ml (2 tbsp) in each pocket. Secure with toothpicks.
4. Braai chops over moderate coals for about 15 minutes until golden-brown. Remove toothpicks and serve immediately.

Breadcrumbs

So easy to make. Take two-day-old bread, cut into small pieces and crumble in a food processor. Alternatively, bake slices of bread in the oven until crisp, then crush with a rolling pin. Store in an airtight container for later use.

SPARE RIBS WITH PEACH SAUCE

SERVES 4–6

1 kg pork spare ribs
MARINADE
60 ml (¼ cup) soya sauce
80 ml (⅓ cup) dry white wine
410 g can peach halves in syrup, liquidized
30 ml (2 tbsp) honey
15 ml (1 tbsp) chopped fresh root ginger
3 cloves garlic, crushed
salt and freshly ground black pepper to taste

1. For marinade: Mix all ingredients and pour over ribs.
2. Cover and marinate in the refrigerator for 4–6 hours, or overnight if preferred.
3. Braai ribs over moderate coals for 15–20 minutes, basting frequently with the marinade until golden-brown. Cut into portions.
4. Warm remaining marinade and serve with the ribs.

PORK ROAST
(FOR KETTLE BRAAI ONLY)

SERVES 8–10

± 2.8 kg leg of pork
BASTING SAUCE
125 ml (½ cup) peach or orange juice
30 ml (2 tbsp) honey
30 ml (2 tbsp) fresh lemon juice
2 ml (¼ tsp) grated lemon rind

1. For basting sauce: Mix all ingredients together.
2. When the coals are ready, place pork on the grid in the kettle. After 1 hour, baste the meat with the sauce.
3. Roast for another hour, basting frequently. Cut off crackling and serve. Leave pork for another 30 minutes until medium- to well-done. Continue basting.

meat

PORK PIN WHEELS

MAKES ABOUT 8

1 kg pork belly, skin removed
10 ml (2 tsp) olive oil
15 ml (1 tbsp) barbecue spice
15 ml (1 tbsp) ground coriander
30 ml (2 tbsp) chopped fresh mixed herbs
or 10 ml (2 tsp) dried
salt and freshly ground black pepper to taste

1. Brush pork belly with oil. Mix all remaining ingredients together and sprinkle over belly.
2. Roll up and secure with skewers at 25 mm intervals. Cut into slices to make wheels.
3. Braai wheels over moderate coals for 15–20 minutes, or until done.

KEBABS WITH PEPPADEWS

MAKES 6

350 g pork cubes (cut from leg), 25 mm thick
1 medium green pepper, seeded and cut into 25 mm cubes
6 pickling onions, peeled and halved
200 g canned peppadews in syrup (about 18)
BASTING SAUCE
80 ml (⅓ cup) syrup from canned peppadews
10 ml (2 tsp) honey
15 ml (1 tbsp) light brown sugar
salt and freshly ground black pepper to taste

1. Thread the pork onto skewers, alternating with green pepper, onion and peppadews.
2. For basting sauce: Mix all ingredients together.
3. Braai kebabs over moderate coals for 15–20 minutes, turning and basting frequently with the sauce until done.

DELICIOUS SAGE CHOPS

Classic sage is still the best combination with pork.

SERVES 6

6 pork loin chops, 20 mm thick
30 ml (2 tbsp) olive oil
BASTING SAUCE
125 ml (½ cup) fresh lemon juice
30 ml (2 tbsp) chopped fresh sage or 10 ml (2 tsp) dried
salt and freshly ground black pepper to taste

1. Trim excess fat from chops, then slash edges of remaining fat at 25 mm intervals.
2. For basting sauce: Mix lemon juice, sage and seasoning.
3. Brush chops with olive oil.
4. Braai chops over moderate coals for about 20 minutes, turning and basting frequently with the sauce until done.

Sage

This herb goes well with pork because the slightly bitter flavour breaks down the fatty taste. It combines with marjoram and thyme to make mixed herbs. Fresh sage will keep for up to a week in the refrigerator. If dried, stored in an airtight container and kept away from sunlight, it can keep for several months.

FROM TOP TO BOTTOM: *Pork Pin Wheels, Kebabs with Peppadews, Delicious Sage Chops (see page 54).*

meat 55

SMOKED PORK CHOPS WITH MANGO

SERVES 4

4 pork rib chops, 20 mm thick
30 ml (2 tbsp) olive oil
10 ml (2 tsp) barbecue spice
freshly ground black pepper to taste
425 g can mangoes, puréed

1. Trim excess fat from chops, then slash edges of remaining fat at 25 mm intervals.
2. Brush chops with oil on both sides and sprinkle with spice and pepper.
3. Cover the bottom of a flat cast-iron pot (No. 12) with sawdust, then top with a rack (a cooling rack can be used). Place the pot over moderate coals and arrange the chops on the rack. Cover with lid.
4. Leave to smoke for 10–12 minutes until golden-brown. Remove from pot and serve with chilled mango purée.

CHOPS WITH PINEAPPLE AND GINGER

SERVES 4

4 pork rib or loin chops, 20 mm thick
440 g can pineapple slices, drained or
1 small pineapple, sliced
30 ml (2 tbsp) light brown sugar
2 ml (¼ tsp) ground ginger
5 ml (1 tsp) grated lemon rind

1. Trim excess fat from chops, then slash edges of remaining fat at 25 mm intervals.
2. Heat a cast-iron plate over moderate coals or use a skottel. Place chops on the plate and brown on one side.
3. Place pineapple slices on the plate. Mix sugar, ginger and rind and sprinkle over both sides of pineapple.
4. Braai chops for about 10 minutes, turning until cooked, then serve with the pineapple.

RIB CHOPS WITH AVOCADO SAUCE

This delicious and versatile sauce can also be served as a dip.

SERVES 8

8 pork rib chops, 20 mm thick
salt and freshly ground black pepper to taste

AVOCADO SAUCE

1 medium avocado, finely mashed
20 ml (4 tsp) lemon juice
5 ml (1 tsp) finely grated lemon rind
125 ml (½ cup) plain, unflavoured yoghurt
2 ml (¼ tsp) salt
2 ml (¼ tsp) Tabasco sauce

1. For sauce: Mix all ingredients together and chill for at least 30 minutes.
2. Trim excess fat from chops, then slash edges of remaining fat at 25 mm intervals.
3. Braai pork chops over moderate coals for about 20 minutes, or until cooked. Season, then serve with cold avocado sauce.

Variation

Substitute avocado with a can of peaches, apricots or mangoes, drained and puréed.

Whole-grain mustard
This mustard contains a mixture of white and brown mustard seeds which have been preserved in white wine vinegar and sugar.

HONEY-GLAZED PORK FILLET

SERVES 4–6

600 g pork fillet

GLAZE

30 ml (2 tbsp) chopped root ginger
60 ml (¼ cup) honey
30 ml (2 tbsp) medium cream sherry
60 ml (¼ cup) fresh lemon juice
5 ml (1 tsp) grated lemon rind
salt and freshly ground black pepper to taste

1. For glaze: Mix all ingredients together and set aside.
2. Braai fillet over moderate coals for about 10 minutes. Turn, then glaze and braai for another 10 minutes. Serve immediately.

Tip
When honey becomes crystallized, place the jar in hot water to dissolve the crystals.

SAUSAGES WRAPPED IN BACON

SERVES 6

6 pork sausages
100 g Cheddar cheese, cut into strips
125 g rindless streaky bacon

GLAZE

15 ml (1 tbsp) honey
5 ml (1 tsp) whole-grain mustard

1. Braai sausages over moderate coals for about 10 minutes, until they start to brown. Remove from coals.
2. Use a sharp knife to cut them lengthwise, almost through to the bottom. Fill with cheese and use finger pressure to close tightly.
3. Wrap with bacon and secure with toothpicks. Braai over moderate coals for a further 5–10 minutes, turning and basting frequently with the glaze until done.

FROM LEFT TO RIGHT: *Sausages wrapped in Bacon, Honey-glazed Pork Fillet.*

meat 57

venison

BUTTERMILK STEAKS

SERVES 6

6 venison steaks (± 350 g), 20 mm thick

MARINADE

250 ml (1 cup) buttermilk
15 ml (1 tbsp) fresh lemon juice
2 cloves garlic, crushed
1 onion, sliced
2 bay leaves
15 ml (1 tbsp) chopped fresh thyme
or 5 ml (1 tsp) dried
salt and freshly ground black pepper to taste

1. For marinade: Mix all ingredients together.
2. Cover steaks with marinade and place in the refrigerator for 2–3 hours, or overnight if preferred.
3. Remove steaks from marinade and braai over moderate coals for 12–15 minutes, or until cooked.

Bay leaves

Dried or fresh leaves can be used, but set aside fresh leaves for a day or two to reduce the bitterness. To dry the leaves, hang up a twig or branch out of direct sunlight and in a dry place for about two weeks. Whole leaves are added to dishes to enhance the flavour and should be removed before serving. Use only one or two leaves at a time as the flavour is quite strong and can spoil a dish.

FINE SHREDDED VENISON

SERVES 6–8

4 kg venison stewing meat
3 onions, chopped
4 cloves garlic, peeled
salt and freshly ground black pepper to taste

MARINADE

150 g spek (fat)
45 ml (3 tbsp) fresh lemon juice
30 ml (2 tbsp) cooking oil
4 bay leaves
6 cloves garlic, peeled
250 ml (1 cup) dry red wine
375 ml (1½ cups) red wine vinegar

1. For marinade: Mix all ingredients together. Place meat in a large bowl and cover with marinade. Leave to marinate for 2–3 days.
2. Place a large cast-iron pot (No. 12) on a grid over hot coals. Heat oil and sauté onions and garlic until soft. Add meat and marinade to onions. Season. Cover and simmer for about 2½ hours.
3. Remove pot from heat and spoon out meat. Leave meat to cool slightly and remove all bones. Reserve 250 ml (1 cup) of liquid. Add meat and reserved liquid to pot and cook again over moderate coals for about 30 minutes while stirring frequently to form a fine mixture.
4. Serve with rice or potatoes.

VENISON SADDLE WITH WINE BASTE (FOR KETTLE BRAAI ONLY)

SERVES 4–6

± 800 g loin saddle
WINE BASTE (see page 22)

1. When the coals reach moderate heat, place the saddle on the grid in the kettle and close the lid.
2. Braai for about 50 minutes, basting frequently with the wine baste until cooked.

58 on the coals

Venison saddle (see page 58).

VENISON SAUSAGE

MAKES ABOUT 3.5 KG

1.5 kg venison, cut into 25 mm cubes
1.5 kg mutton, cut into 25 mm cubes
500 g mutton fat, cut into 5 mm cubes
60 ml (¼ cup) whole coriander
30 ml (2 tbsp) salt
3 ml (½ tsp) freshly ground black pepper
3 ml (½ tsp) ground cloves
2 ml (¼ tsp) ground nutmeg
10 ml (2 tsp) chopped fresh thyme or 3 ml (½ tsp) dried
80 ml (⅓ cup) vinegar or red wine
30 ml (2 tbsp) Worcestershire sauce
± 100 g pork or mutton casing

1. Layer all meat and fat in a large dish.
2. Sear coriander in a heavy-based saucepan over medium heat. Leave to cool and grind well. Sift to remove husks.
3. Mix all dry ingredients together and sprinkle over meat and fat. Mix well.
4. Add vinegar and Worcestershire sauce to meat and mix well.
5. Fill casing and leave for at least 24 hours in the refrigerator to allow the flavours of the spices and vinegar to develop. The sausage can be frozen for up to 2 months.
6. Braai over moderate-low coals for about 20 minutes for well-done.

fish & seafood

SALMON STEAKS WITH BASIL

SERVES 4

4 salmon steaks, 25 mm thick
lemon wedges

MARINADE

80 ml (⅓ cup) olive oil
45 ml (3 tbsp) balsamic vinegar
5 ml (1 tsp) soya sauce
2 ml (¼ tsp) Worcestershire sauce
30 ml (2 tbsp) chopped fresh basil or 10 ml (2 tsp) dried
salt and freshly ground black pepper to taste

1. For marinade: Mix all ingredients and pour over fish. Cover and leave to marinate for 30 minutes.
2. Remove salmon and place in an oiled, hinged grid over moderate coals for 10–15 minutes, turning and basting frequently with the marinade until cooked.
3. Serve immediately with lemon wedges.

Variation

HONEY AND ORANGE GLAZE

30 ml (2 tbsp) finely chopped root ginger
20 ml (4 tsp) honey
80 ml (⅓ cup) orange juice

Mix all ingredients together and baste salmon steaks frequently until the fish is cooked through.

Basil

This soft, leafy herb is only available fresh seasonally. It can, however, be preserved in oil. Alternatively, make pesto (see page 36) when basil is available and freeze it for later use.

FISH IN BANANA LEAVES

Most fish is delicious when cooked wrapped in leaves. Fig, vine, citrus and banana leaves all keep food moist and impart their own flavour. Secure the parcels with fine string, toothpicks or bamboo skewers.

SERVES 4–6

1 large fish or a few small ones
(any fish such as red roman or even hake)
banana leaves
lemon wedges

TOPPING

3 cloves garlic, crushed
1 red chilli, seeded and chopped
10 ml (2 tsp) hot chilli sauce
30 ml (2 tbsp) olive oil
30 ml (2 tbsp) chopped fresh mixed herbs or 10 ml (2 tsp) dried
60 ml (¼ cup) fresh lemon juice
salt and freshly ground black pepper to taste

1. Use a sharp knife to cut a few deep diagonal cuts into the skin on both sides of fish.
2. For topping: Mix all ingredients together and spread over both sides of fish.
3. Place fish on a large piece of banana leaf. Wrap up tightly and secure with skewers.
4. Braai over moderate coals for 20–25 minutes depending on the size of fish, turning halfway through cooking time. Serve with lemon wedges.

RIGHT, FROM TOP TO BOTTOM: *Salmon Steaks with Basil, Fish in Banana Leaves.*

on the coals

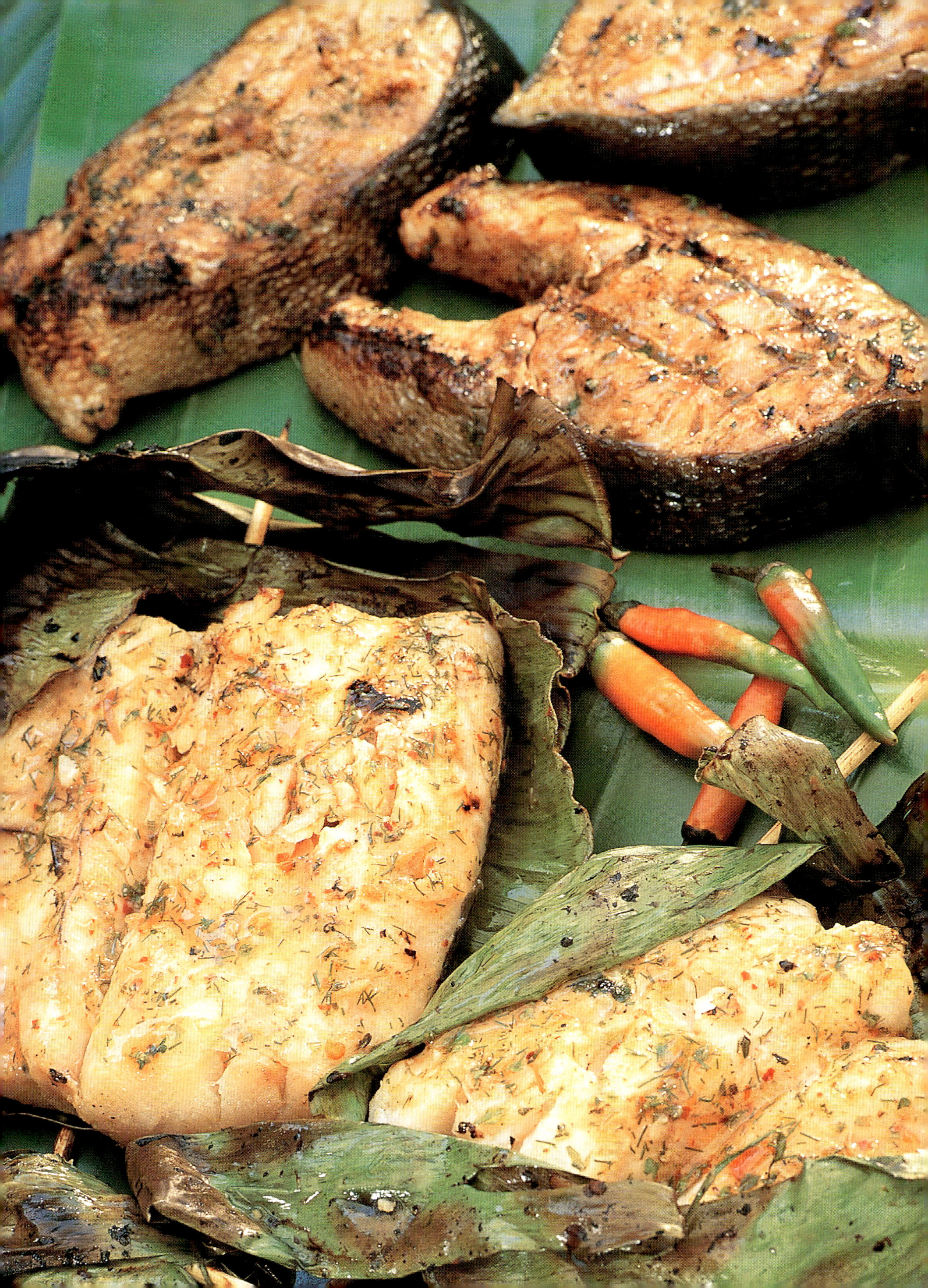

FROM TOP TO BOTTOM: *Grilled Kabeljou with Cashew Nut Filling, Orange and Dill Trout (see page 63).*

TUNA AND PEPPER KEBABS

Use any fresh vegetables for a colourful presentation.

MAKES ABOUT 6

500 g tuna or salmon fillets, cut into 25 mm cubes
1 green pepper, seeded and cut into 25 mm cubes
1 red or yellow pepper, seeded and
cut into 25 mm cubes
12 cherry tomatoes
lemon wedges

BASTING SAUCE

60 ml (¼ cup) olive oil
30 ml (2 tbsp) fresh lemon juice
5 ml (1 tsp) honey
1 clove garlic, crushed
10 ml (2 tsp) chopped fresh dill or 3 ml (½ tsp) dried

1. Thread the fish cubes onto skewers, alternating with peppers and tomatoes.
2. For basting sauce: Mix all ingredients together.
3. Braai kebabs over moderate coals for 15–20 minutes, turning and basting frequently until done. Serve with lemon wedges.

> Sweet peppers
> Originally only green and red peppers were available, but now orange, yellow, white and purple peppers are also obtainable. The flavour of red, orange and yellow peppers is sweeter than the green, which is unripe.

ORANGE AND DILL TROUT

The combination of orange and dill is excellent, but other soft herbs such as fennel, marjoram or thyme can also be used.

SERVES 4–6

1 large whole trout (± 800 g) or 6 small trout, cleaned and gutted
coarse salt
1 orange, sliced
lemon wedges

MARINADE

125 ml (½ cup) orange juice
10 ml (2 tsp) grated orange rind
60 ml (¼ cup) olive oil
15 ml (1 tbsp) whole-grain mustard
15 ml (1 tbsp) sugar
60 ml (¼ cup) chopped fresh dill or 20 ml (4 tsp) dried
salt and freshly ground black pepper to taste

1. Sprinkle coarse salt on the inside and outside of fish and leave to stand for 30 minutes. Rinse off salt and pat dry. Use a sharp knife to slash a few deep diagonal cuts into the skin on both sides.
2. For marinade: Mix all ingredients together.
3. Place orange slices in the cavity of the fish, cover and marinate in the refrigerator for about 1 hour, turning occasionally.
4. Remove trout and place in an oiled, hinged grid over moderate coals for 30–40 minutes, turning and basting frequently with marinade until fish is cooked.
5. Season with more salt if necessary and serve with lemon wedges.

Dill
This tall annual plant with feathery leaves is related to parsley and is particularly useful for garnishing.

Tip
Slash the skin of the fish on the thickest part of the body to ensure even grilling. If the fish is being marinated, make slashes before placing the fish in the marinade to flavour and tenderize the meat.

GRILLED KABELJOU (KOB) WITH CASHEW NUT FILLING

Luxurious filling, but worth it!

SERVES 6

2 whole kabeljou (± 700 g each), cleaned and gutted
coarse salt
lemon wedges

FILLING

1 onion, finely chopped
1 medium green pepper, chopped
2 cloves garlic, crushed
50 g butter
100 g cashew nuts, coarsely chopped
125 ml (½ cup) freshly prepared brown or white breadcrumbs
15 ml (1 tbsp) chopped fresh mixed herbs or 5 ml (1 tsp) dried
30 ml (2 tbsp) fresh lemon juice
5 ml (1 tsp) grated lemon rind
salt and freshly ground black pepper to taste

BASTING SAUCE

250 g black pepper butter (see page 93)

1. Sprinkle coarse salt on the inside and outside of fish. Leave to stand for about 30 minutes. Rinse off salt and pat dry. Use a sharp knife to slash a few deep diagonal cuts into the skin on both sides.
2. For filling: Sauté the onion, green pepper and garlic until soft. Stir in nuts and breadcrumbs. Add remaining ingredients.
3. Stuff the fish with the nut mixture and secure the opening with wooden or metal skewers so that the filling does not fall out.
4. Place the fish in an oiled, hinged grid over moderate coals and grill for 15–20 minutes, turning and basting frequently with pepper butter on both sides. Do not press down too hard when turning the fish as you could damage the skin. Serve with lemon wedges.

Variation
Substitute cashew nuts with any other nuts of choice.

fish & seafood

PRAWN KEBABS WITH MINT AND PARMESAN CHEESE

Easy to make and very colourful.

MAKES 10–12

30 uncooked prawns (± 350 g)
2 small lemons
16 mange-tout
BASTING SAUCE
60 g butter
45 ml (3 tbsp) fresh lemon juice
15 ml (1 tbsp) chopped fresh mint or 5 ml (1 tsp) dried
30 ml (2 tbsp) finely grated Parmesan cheese
salt and freshly ground black pepper to taste

1. For basting sauce: Melt butter, add lemon juice and leave to cool slightly. Add remaining ingredients.
2. Cut each lemon into 6 wedges. Blanch the mange-tout to soften slightly. Thread the prawns onto skewers, alternating with the lemon wedges and mange-tout.
3. Braai kebabs over moderate coals for 10–12 minutes, turning and basting frequently with the sauce.

Tip
It is preferable to devein prawns before cooking them. If the digestive tube is large and black, cut a slit along the back of the prawn and pull out the vein.

GRILLED SARDINES

SERVES 6

18 fresh whole sardines
coarse sea salt
lemon wedges

1. Remove scales under water by scraping them off with a knife. Sprinkle fish with salt.
2. Place fish in an oiled, hinged grid and braai over moderate-hot coals for 8–10 minutes until crisp. Serve with lemon wedges.

KINGKLIP WITH SUN-DRIED TOMATO MARINADE

SERVES 4

4 kingklip fillet steaks (± 330 g)
MARINADE
60 ml (¼ cup) olive oil
45 ml (3 tbsp) fresh lemon juice
25 g sun-dried tomatoes (± 10), soaked in water and chopped
10 ml (2 tsp) sugar
1 clove garlic, crushed
10 ml (2 tsp) chopped fresh thyme or 3 ml (½ tsp) dried
salt and freshly ground black pepper to taste

1. For marinade: Mix all ingredients together and pour over fish. Leave to marinate for 30 minutes.
2. Remove fish and place in an oiled, hinged grid over moderate coals. Turn and baste the fish frequently with marinade for 15–20 minutes. Serve immediately.

Variation
Omit the marinade and serve the kingklip with lemon-garlic butter (see page 93).

GRILLED YELLOWTAIL WITH ROSEMARY BASTE

1 whole yellowtail (± 800 g), cleaned and gutted
coarse salt
lemon wedges
ROSEMARY BASTE (see page 22)

1. Prepare basting sauce, but substitute rosemary for chopped fresh marjoram or origanum.
2. Fleck fish open. Sprinkle coarse salt on the inside and outside and leave to stand for about 30 minutes. Rinse off salt and pat dry.
3. Place fish, skin-side down, in an oiled, hinged grid over moderate coals. Grill for 25–30 minutes, basting frequently. Grill the flesh side last. Serve immediately with lemon wedges.

FROM TOP TO BOTTOM: *Prawn Kebabs with Mint and Parmesan Cheese, Grilled Yellowtail (see page 64).*

fish & seafood 65

ANGEL FISH WITH MUSTARD BASTE

SERVES 6–8

1 whole angel fish (± 2 kg), cleaned and gutted
coarse salt
lemon wedges

BASTING SAUCE

30 ml (2 tbsp) chopped fresh fennel or 5 ml (1 tsp) dried
200 ml (¾ cup) fresh lemon juice
80 ml (⅓ cup) olive oil
30 ml (2 tbsp) whole-grain mustard
2 cloves garlic, crushed
salt and freshly ground black pepper to taste

1. Sprinkle coarse salt on the inside and outside of fish and leave to stand for about 30 minutes. Rinse off salt and pat dry. Use a sharp knife to slash a few deep diagonal cuts into the skin on both sides.
2. For basting sauce: Mix all ingredients together.
3. Place fish in an oiled, hinged grid over moderate coals for 30–35 minutes. Grill until golden-brown on both sides, turning and basting frequently. Serve immediately with lemon wedges.

Fennel
This herb has a mild aniseed-type flavour that becomes milder with cooking. It has green feathery leaves with clusters of tiny yellow flowers and is most often used with fish, pork or in salads.

Tartare sauce

250 ml (1 cup) mayonnaise
2 eggs, hard-boiled and finely chopped
15 ml (1 tbsp) finely chopped gherkins
1 small onion, finely chopped
15 ml (1 tbsp) chopped fresh parsley or 5 ml (1 tsp) dried
5 ml (1 tsp) chopped fresh tarragon or 2 ml (¼ tsp) dried

Mix all ingredients together.
Cover and refrigerate until needed.

SOLE IN CREAMY MUSHROOM SAUCE

SERVES 2

2 medium soles (± 250 g each)
60 g butter
5 spring onions, chopped
60 ml (¼ cup) dry white wine
125 g button mushrooms
30 ml (2 tbsp) fresh lemon juice
60 ml (¼ cup) fresh cream
salt and freshly ground black pepper to taste

1. Start at the tail end and lift the skin. Sprinkle fish with salt, leave to stand a few minutes, then rinse off salt.
2. Place a flat cast-iron pot (No. 10) over hot coals. Heat butter and seal soles on both sides.
3. Add spring onions and sauté lightly. Add wine, mushrooms and lemon juice and simmer with the fish for 8–10 minutes.
4. Add cream and seasoning. Serve immediately.

CALAMARI IN GARLIC

SERVES 4–6

80 g butter
2–4 cloves garlic, crushed
500 g calamari rings
15 ml (1 tbsp) chopped fresh parsley or 5 ml (1 tsp) dried
5 ml (1 tsp) grated lemon rind
60 ml (¼ cup) fresh lemon juice
salt and freshly ground black pepper to taste

1. Place a flat cast-iron plate over hot coals. Heat butter and sauté garlic lightly.
2. Add calamari rings and fry quickly for about 3 minutes.
3. Add parsley, lemon rind, juice and seasoning. Serve immediately with tartare sauce on the side.

Lemon juice
To get more juice out of lemons, heat them for a few minutes in the microwave or oven before squeezing.

GRILLED CRAYFISH

The flesh cooks in the time that it takes for the shells to turn bright red.

SERVES 6

6 fresh crayfish tails
BASTING SAUCE
125 g lemon-garlic butter (see page 93)
80 ml (⅓ cup) fresh lemon juice
salt and freshly ground black pepper to taste

1. Split through the shell of the crayfish using kitchen scissors or a sharp knife, and remove the head sac, intestines and vein. Rinse and dry.
2. For basting sauce: Melt butter and add remaining ingredients.
3. Place crayfish flesh-side down over moderate coals and grill for about 1 minute. Turn and grill for a further 10–12 minutes, basting frequently with sauce until tail meat is white. Serve immediately.

Tip
Test for freshness by pulling back the crayfish tail. If fresh, it should immediately slip back into a curled position.

HAKE IN FOIL

SERVES 4–6

6 hake fillet steaks (± 250 g each)
2 onions, sliced
2 tomatoes, sliced
100 g herb butter (see page 93)
salt and freshly ground black pepper to taste
45 ml (3 tbsp) fresh lemon juice

1. Place each fillet in a double layer of foil, about 30 x 30 cm. Top with onion and tomato slices. Dot with herb butter and season.
2. Drizzle with lemon juice before closing each parcel.
3. Braai over moderate coals for 20–25 minutes.

GRILLED SNOEK WITH APRICOT BASTE

SERVES 6

1 whole snoek, (± 1.8 kg)
coarse salt
lemon wedges
BASTING SAUCE
80 g butter
125 ml (½ cup) smooth apricot jam
60 ml (¼ cup) fresh lemon juice
2 ml (¼ tsp) grated lemon rind
1 clove garlic, crushed

1. Fleck fish open. Sprinkle salt on the inside and outside of fish and leave to stand for about 30 minutes. Rinse off salt and pat dry.
2. For basting sauce: Melt butter and add remaining ingredients.
3. Place fish, skin-side down, in a well-oiled, hinged grid over moderate coals. Grill for 20–25 minutes, basting frequently. Grill flesh side last. Serve immediately with lemon wedges.

Variation
Substitute apricot jam with moskonfyt. Alternatively baste fish with 125 g lemon-garlic butter (see page 93).

Hints when braaiing fish
- Fish is tender and only needs a short period in marinade to add flavour. The marinade should not overpower the natural fish flavour.
- Flat, hinged wire baskets are convenient for turning delicate or smaller fish. For best results, oil the grill lightly before you start to prevent the fish from sticking.
- Fish cooks quickly over moderate heat. It will sear the outside and cook the inside. Long, slow cooking will result in dry fish that falls apart. Thick dense fish fillets, such as tuna and sword fish, grill well over high heat, while more delicate fish (salmon and trout) cooks best over medium-hot coals.
- Use a large spatula or tongs to turn fish. Don't turn repeatedly or it may fall apart.

poultry

LEMON-PEPPER SPATCHCOCK CHICKEN

An interesting way to serve a whole chicken.

SERVES 4–6

1 whole chicken (about 1.4 kg)
MARINADE
125 ml (½ cup) fresh lemon juice
10 ml (2 tsp) grated lemon rind
80 ml (⅓ cup) olive oil
2 cloves garlic, crushed
5 ml (1 tsp) salt
10 ml (2 tsp) freshly ground coarse black pepper

1. Use a sharp knife or kitchen scissors to cut the chicken along the centre back, from neck to tail. Trim excess fat from chicken. Place chicken on a cutting board, skin-side up, and press down firmly with heel of hand to flatten. Make a few deep diagonal cuts into the skin.
2. For marinade: Combine all ingredients in a large dish and mix well. Add chicken, cover and leave to marinate in the refrigerator for 4–6 hours, or overnight if preferred.
3. Remove chicken from marinade and braai over moderate coals for 40–45 minutes, or until cooked. Serve immediately.

Olive oil

Different grades of olive oil are available. Extra-virgin oil is obtained from the first cold pressing and is the most flavoursome and aromatic. It also has the lowest smoking point and is best for salads and uncooked food. Virgin olive oil can be used for cooking as it stands up to heat better. Do not refrigerate olive oil as it will solidify. Store in a cool, dark place for up to two years.

STUFFED SUN-DRIED TOMATO CHICKEN BREASTS

SERVES 8

8 deboned, skinned chicken breasts
FILLING
25 g (± 10) sun-dried tomatoes
150 g spinach leaves, shredded
10 ml (2 tsp) sugar
100 g Feta cheese, crumbled
15 ml (1 tbsp) chopped fresh mixed herbs
or 5 ml (1 tsp) dried
salt and freshly ground black pepper to taste

1. Use a sharp knife to cut a horizontal slit in the thick section of each breast, making a pocket for filling.
2. For filling: Soak sun-dried tomatoes for a few minutes in enough hot water to cover. Drain and cut into smaller pieces.
3. Blanch spinach until soft and combine with tomatoes and all remaining ingredients.
4. Place spoonfuls of filling in each pocket and secure with toothpicks.
5. Braai over moderate coals for 15–20 minutes until cooked through. Serve immediately.

Sun-dried tomatoes

Make your own: Cut ripe plum tomatoes in half and place cut-side up on a wire rack. Sprinkle with salt and bake in a preheated oven at 100 °C (200 °F) for 5–6 hours until dried out.

RIGHT: *Lemon-Pepper Spatchcock Chicken*

on the coals

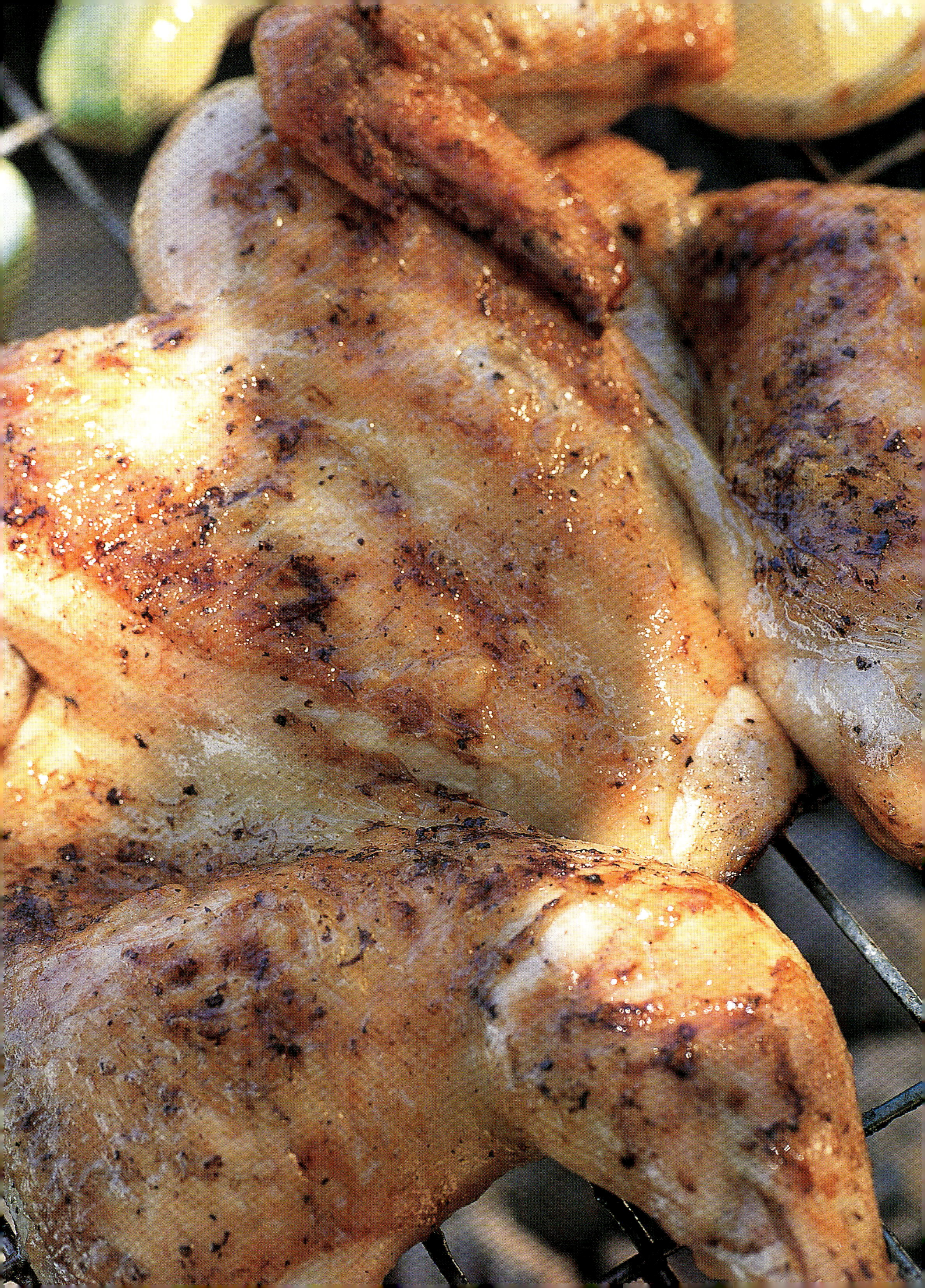

Roast Chicken (see page 71)

**ROAST DUCK WITH ORANGE AND GINGER
(FOR KETTLE BRAAI ONLY)**

SERVES 4–6

2.2 kg duck
2.5 cm piece root ginger, peeled
salt and freshly ground black pepper to taste
BASTING SAUCE
15 ml (1 tbsp) butter
20 ml (4 tsp) finely chopped fresh root ginger
60 ml (¼ cup) orange juice
5 ml (1 tsp) grated orange rind
15 ml (1 tbsp) medium cream sherry
salt and freshly ground black pepper to taste

1. Remove all excess fat from inside of duck. Rub the piece of ginger inside the cavity and leave it inside. Season with salt and pepper. Truss duck with string.
2. For basting sauce: Melt butter, then add remaining ingredients.
3. Place duck on a grid with hot coals on the sides of the kettle. Baste duck frequently and cook for about 1½ hours until golden-brown.

Variation
Omit the ginger and orange and serve duck with green peppercorn sauce (see page 32).

70 on the coals

SWEET-AND-SOUR KEBABS

MAKES ABOUT 12

4 deboned, skinned chicken breasts,
cut into 25 mm cubes
250 g pitted prunes
440 g can pineapple pieces, juice reserved
125 g dried apricots

PINEAPPLE SAUCE

200 ml (¾ cup) reserved pineapple juice
30 ml (2 tbsp) vinegar
10 ml (2 tsp) soya sauce
15 ml (1 tbsp) light brown sugar
2 ml (¼ tsp) ground ginger
15 ml (1 tbsp) cornflour

1. Thread the chicken cubes onto skewers, alternating with prunes, pineapple pieces and apricots.
2. For pineapple sauce: Mix all ingredients in a heavy-based saucepan. Stir constantly and boil for 2–3 minutes until thickened. Set aside.
3. Braai kebabs over moderate coals for 15–20 minutes, turning and basting frequently with the sauce. Heat remaining sauce and serve with kebabs.

> **Tip**
> To make flavoured vinegar: Place fresh herbs, such as rosemary, tarragon, thyme, marjoram, in a bottle and add good quality vinegar. Store for about 3 weeks before using in salad dressings, mayonnaise or marinades.

ROAST CHICKEN
(FOR KETTLE BRAAI ONLY)

SERVES 4–6

1 chicken (± 1.3 kg) or 2 poussins
salt and freshly ground black pepper to taste
4 sprigs rosemary
20 ml (4 tsp) butter
20 ml (4 tsp) olive oil
125 g rindless streaky bacon

1. Remove giblets and trim excess fat. Season the chicken cavity with salt and pepper. Place two sprigs of rosemary inside the cavity. Alternatively, use garlic, onion and lemon slices. Truss the chicken with string.
2. Heat butter and oil in a small saucepan and brush chicken with half of this mixture.
3. Place chicken on a grid with hot coals on sides of kettle. Cover and cook for about 15 minutes. Open, baste with remaining butter and oil. Cover with strips of bacon, covering as much of the surface as possible. Place the two remaining sprigs of rosemary on top.
4. Close lid and cook chicken for a further 50–60 minutes.

TURKEY DRUMSTICKS

SERVES 4

1 turkey drumstick (± 650 g), cut into 6 steaks

MARINADE

15 ml (1 tbsp) ground coriander
2 ml (¼ tsp) ground ginger
3 ml (½ tsp) cayenne pepper
80 ml (⅓ cup) olive oil
125 ml (½ cup) fresh lemon juice

1. For marinade: Mix all ingredients together.
2. Cover turkey steaks with marinade and place in the refrigerator for 4–6 hours, or overnight if preferred.
3. Braai steaks over moderate-low coals, brushing frequently with marinade for 35–40 minutes, or until golden-brown and crisp.

TROPICAL HONEY CHICKEN

The rich flavour is sure to make this dish a winner at any braai.

SERVES 6

8 chicken pieces (drumsticks, thighs or breasts)
BASTING SAUCE
125 ml (½ cup) pineapple juice
60 ml (¼ cup) honey
5 ml (1 tsp) chopped fresh marjoram
or 2 ml (¼ tsp) dried
2 ml (¼ tsp) ground ginger
salt and freshly ground black pepper to taste
10 ml (2 tsp) cake flour

1. Trim excess fat from chicken pieces.
2. For basting sauce: Use a medium heavy-based saucepan and combine all ingredients. Bring to the boil and simmer for a few minutes until thickened. Set aside.
3. Braai chicken over moderate coals for about 20 minutes, turning and basting occasionally with the sauce until dark brown. Watch it closely as it burns easily.
4. Heat remaining sauce (thicken by mixing flour with a little water) and serve with chicken.

Variation
Use apple or apricot juice instead of pineapple.

Marjoram
Marjoram has small oval leaves with a spicy, sweet flavour. Two varieties, sweet and wild, are available. Marjoram usually applies to the sweet, while the wild variety is commonly referred to as origanum.

Origanum

PARMESAN CHICKEN

SERVES 6

8 chicken drumsticks, skinned
60 ml (¼ cup) cake flour
5 ml (1 tsp) salt
freshly ground black pepper to taste
2 eggs, beaten
250 ml (1 cup) freshly prepared brown
or white breadcrumbs
80 ml (⅓ cup) finely grated Parmesan cheese

1. Season the flour with salt and pepper and coat the chicken.
2. Dip chicken in beaten eggs.
3. Mix breadcrumbs and Parmesan cheese and roll drumsticks in the mix. Apply light finger pressure to ensure chicken is well coated. Chill in refrigerator for at least 30 minutes.
4. Braai over moderate coals for 15–20 minutes, turning carefully with tongs. Serve hot or cold.

Tip
Before cooking, place crumbed food in the refrigerator for at least 30 minutes to prevent the crumbs from falling off during cooking.

OSTRICH STEAKS

SERVES 6

6 ostrich steaks, 20 mm thick
YOGHURT MARINADE (see page 21)
15 ml (1 tbsp) chopped fresh origanum
or 5 ml (1 tsp) dried

1. For marinade: Add origanum to the yoghurt marinade.
2. Cover steaks with marinade and place in the refrigerator for 4–6 hours, or overnight if preferred.
3. Remove steaks from marinade and braai over moderate coals for 12–15 minutes, turning and basting frequently until cooked.

FROM TOP TO BOTTOM: *Tropical Honey Chicken, Parmesan Chicken (see page 72)*.

poultry 73

PERI-PERI SPATCHCOCK CHICKEN

Peri-peri flavour can be varied to suit personal tastes.

SERVES 4–6

1 whole chicken (± 1.4 kg)

MARINADE

80 ml (⅓ cup) fresh lemon juice
125 ml (½ cup) olive oil
10 ml (2 tsp) peri-peri powder
5 ml (1 tsp) hot chilli sauce
2 cloves garlic, crushed
salt and freshly ground black pepper to taste

1. Use a sharp knife or kitchen scissors to cut the chicken along the centre back, from neck to tail. Trim excess fat from chicken. Place chicken on a cutting board, skin-side up, and press down firmly with heel of hand to flatten. Make a few deep diagonal cuts into the skin.
2. For marinade: Combine all ingredients in a large dish, mixing well. Add chicken, cover and leave to marinate in the refrigerator for 4–6 hours, or overnight if preferred.
3. Remove chicken from marinade and braai over moderate coals for 40–45 minutes. Serve immediately.

Tip
Thread several skewers in criss-crossed fashion through the flesh to hold the chicken flat while it cooks.

Chillies
These are available in a variety of colours and can be used dried or fresh. The strength of both is reduced by removing the seeds. The smaller the chilli, the hotter it will be.

GRILLED SESAME CHICKEN IN GARLIC

Slash the chicken before marinating to allow the flavours to soak through.

SERVES 4–6

6 deboned, skinned chicken breasts

MARINADE

15 ml (1 tbsp) soya sauce
60 ml (¼ cup) fresh lemon juice or dry white wine
5 ml (1 tsp) grated lemon rind
30 ml (2 tbsp) light brown sugar
2 cloves garlic, crushed
2 large sprigs rosemary
2 bay leaves
5 ml (1 tsp) sesame seeds
salt and freshly ground black pepper to taste

1. Flatten chicken slightly with your hands and set aside.
2. For marinade: Mix all ingredients together.
3. Add chicken and turn in the marinade until well coated. Cover and leave to marinate in the refrigerator for at least 1 hour.
4. Remove chicken from marinade and braai over moderate coals for 12–15 minutes, turning and basting occasionally with the marinade until cooked. Serve with char-grilled vegetables (see page 96).

Sesame seeds
These have the nuttiest flavour of all the spices, which can be enhanced by roasting them. The oil produced from the seeds is often used for Chinese cooking, in salads and sprinkled over bread, which is then grilled.

SMOKED CHICKEN BREASTS
(FOR KETTLE BRAAI ONLY)

SERVES 4

4 deboned, skinned chicken breasts
15 ml (1 tbsp) olive oil
30 ml (2 tbsp) fresh lemon juice
salt and freshly ground black pepper to taste
4 sesame or poppy seed rolls
12 baby spinach leaves
1 tomato, sliced
15 ml (1 tbsp) chopped fresh chives or 5 ml (1 tsp) dried

1. Place chicken breasts on a grid with moderate coals and smoking chips on the sides of the kettle.
2. Mix olive oil, lemon juice and seasoning. Brush chicken with mix, turning occasionally. Close kettle and cook for 12–15 minutes until done.
3. Spread a little butter on rolls. Top with spinach, tomato, chicken and chives. Serve with any salad dressing (see page 103).

Chives
Chives belong to the onion family. Their delicate flavour and bright green colour make them ideal as a garnish. It is easier to cut the chives directly over food using a pair of scissors.

Mustard
This is made up of a variety of seeds (black being spicy, brown less spicy and white being bitter), which are mixed with a vinegar blend. French mustard is milder than yellow English mustard, which can be quite hot. It is sold as ready-made pastes in jars.

FLAMED CHICKEN WITH MAYONNAISE

SERVES 6

6 deboned, skinned chicken breasts
MARINADE
125 ml (½ cup) mayonnaise
80 ml (⅓ cup) fruit chutney
10 ml (2 tsp) whole-grain mustard
45 ml (3 tbsp) olive oil
15 ml (1 tbsp) lemon juice
salt and freshly ground black pepper to taste

1. Flatten chicken slightly with your hands and set aside.
2. For marinade: Mix all ingredients together.
3. Add chicken and turn in the marinade until well coated. Cover and leave to marinate for 2–3 hours in refrigerator. Remove chicken and set marinade aside.
4. Char-grill chicken over flames for a few minutes until dark brown in colour. Grill further over moderate coals for 10–12 minutes. Serve immediately.

BARBECUE CHICKEN

SERVES 4–6

8 chicken wings or drumsticks
MARINADE
1 onion, finely chopped
60 ml (¼ cup) tomato sauce
60 ml (¼ cup) white wine vinegar
60 ml (¼ cup) Worcestershire sauce
30 ml (2 tbsp) light brown sugar
5 ml (1 tsp) mustard powder
salt and freshly ground black pepper to taste

1. For marinade: Combine all ingredients and mix well. Add chicken, cover and leave to marinate in the refrigerator for 4–6 hours, or overnight if preferred.
2. Remove chicken from marinade and braai over moderate coals for 12–15 minutes, turning and basting until done.

potjie

MIXED VEGETABLE POT

Any fresh vegetables in season can be used.

SERVES 6–8

30 ml (2 tbsp) butter
15 ml (1 tbsp) olive oil
2 leeks, sliced
3 cloves garlic, crushed
400 g unpeeled baby potatoes
500 g peeled pumpkin or butternut
375 ml (1½ cups) vegetable stock
15 ml (1 tbsp) chopped fresh herbs or 5 ml (1 tsp) dried
salt and freshly ground black pepper to taste
1 aubergine (brinjal), sliced
125 g large brown mushrooms
250 g broccoli florets

1. Place a medium cast-iron pot over moderate coals.
2. Heat butter and oil and sauté leeks and garlic until soft, but not brown.
3. Add potatoes, pumpkin, stock, herbs and seasoning. Cover and simmer over low coals for about 30 minutes.
4. Top with aubergine slices, mushrooms and broccoli and simmer for another 20–25 minutes until vegetables are just soft.

Tip
Place moderate-hot coals on the top of the lid if the vegetables are not cooking fast enough.

Leeks
Another relative of the onion family. The base and leaves should be cleaned before using: cut across the leafy end and wash thoroughly under running water.

UPSIDE-DOWN CHICKEN

Something different from the traditional potjies. Here the heat is distributed from the top.

SERVES 6–8

1 whole chicken (± 1.2 kg)
30 ml (2 tbsp) olive oil
2 onions, sliced
2 cloves garlic, crushed
125 g baby marrows
200 g patty pans, halved
1 butternut, sliced
800 g baby potatoes
250 ml (1 cup) chicken stock
10 ml (2 tsp) chopped fresh thyme or 3 ml (½ tsp) dried
salt and freshly ground black pepper to taste

1. Spatchcock the chicken (see page 68). Char-grill on the inside by placing over the flames for 5–8 minutes, until starting to brown.
2. Place a flat-based cast-iron pot (No. 12) over moderate coals. Heat oil and sauté onions and garlic until soft.
3. Start adding vegetables from the softest to hardest. Add baby marrows, patty pans, butternut and baby potatoes. Pour in stock with thyme and seasoning.
4. Remove pot from coals and place on a flat surface.
5. Top vegetables with chicken, skin-side toward lid. Cover with lid. Stack moderate coals on top, covering lid completely. Leave pot for 1¼ hours. Remove all burnt-out coals from lid before opening and serving.

RIGHT: *Upside-down Chicken*

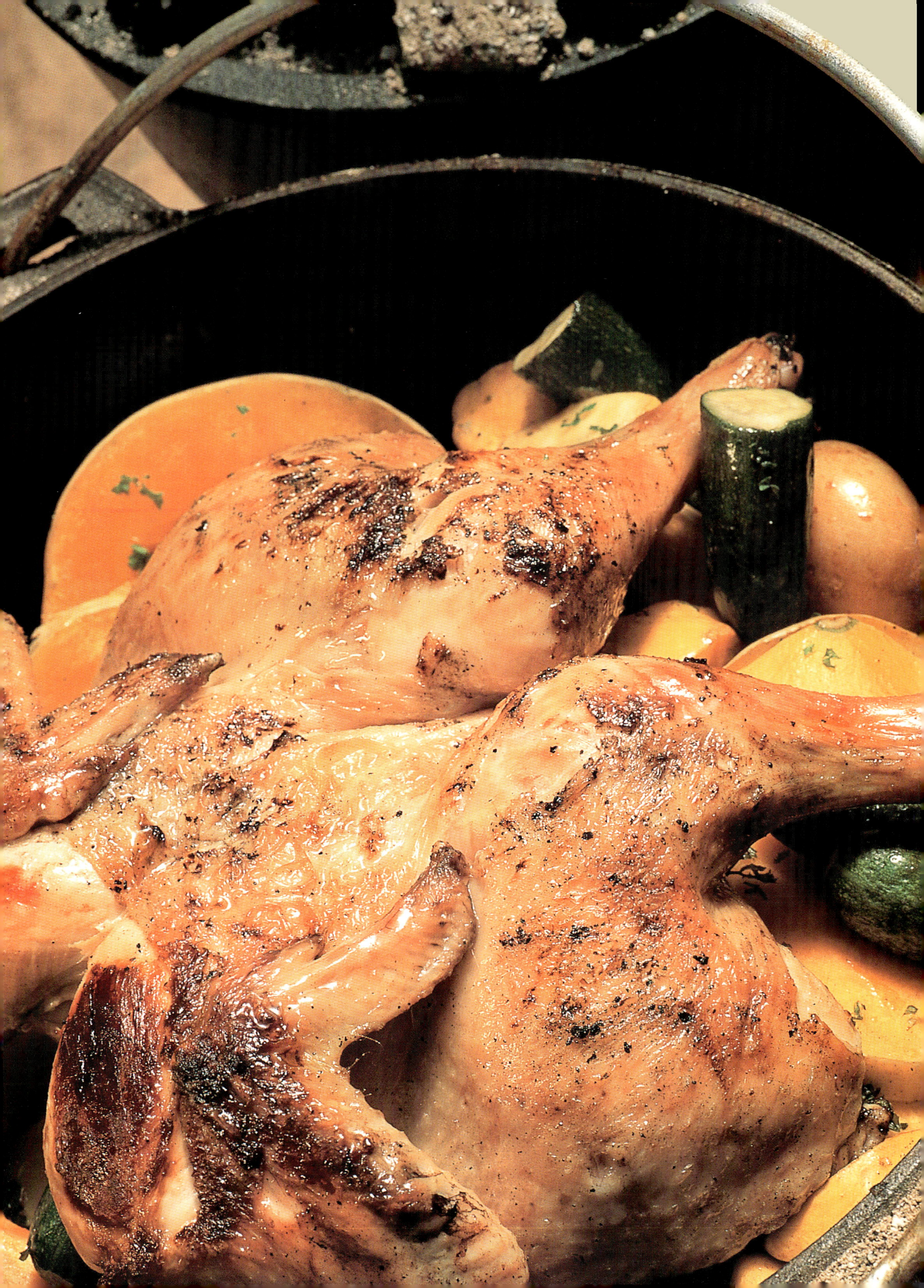

TOMATO LAMB WITH DUMPLINGS

SERVES 6–8

45 ml (3 tbsp) olive oil
1 kg lamb neck slices, 20 mm thick
salt and freshly ground black pepper to taste
3 onions, sliced
2 cloves garlic, crushed
4 tomatoes, skinned and chopped
5 ml (1 tsp) sugar
375 ml (1½ cups) meat stock
3 large potatoes, peeled and quartered

1. Place a cast-iron pot (No. 3) over moderate coals.
2. Heat oil in potjie and fry meat until golden-brown. Add seasoning.
3. Add onions, garlic, tomatoes, sugar and stock and simmer for 1½ hours. Add potatoes, cover and continue to simmer for a further 30 minutes.
4. Prepare dumplings as described below and spoon on top of meat. Cover with lid and leave for about 12 minutes. Serve immediately.

Variation

Substitute tomatoes with ± 200 g fresh waterblommetjies, or 2 cans, and add 15 ml (1 tbsp) lemon juice.

HERB DUMPLINGS

250 ml (1 cup) self-raising flour
5 ml (1 tsp) salt
10 ml (2 tsp) butter
15 ml (1 tbsp) chopped fresh mixed herbs
or 5 ml (1 tsp) dried
1 egg, beaten
60 ml (¼ cup) milk

1. Sift flour and salt. Rub in butter until mixture resembles breadcrumbs. Add herbs.
2. Beat egg and milk together. Mix lightly into flour until just combined.
3. Place tablespoonfuls on top of meat in pot. Do not lift lid for 10 minutes to allow dumplings to cook.

DELICIOUS OXTAIL POTJIE

SERVES 6–8

30 ml (2 tbsp) olive oil
2 oxtails, cut into joints
1 onion, chopped
2 cloves garlic, crushed
2 sticks celery, chopped
125 ml (½ cup) dry red wine
250 ml (1 cup) meat stock
15 ml (1 tbsp) chopped fresh thyme
or 5 ml (1 tsp) dried
15 ml (1 tbsp) chopped fresh rosemary
or 5 ml (1 tsp) dried
salt and freshly ground black pepper to taste
12 pickling onions, peeled
250 g baby carrots
500 g button mushrooms

1. Place a cast-iron pot (No. 3) over moderate coals.
2. Heat oil and fry meat until golden-brown.
3. Add onion, garlic and celery and sauté until soft.
4. Add wine, stock, herbs and seasoning. Simmer over low coals for about 2½ hours.
5. Add pickling onions, carrots and mushrooms and continue to simmer for another 30 minutes.

Celery

Celery can be eaten either raw in salads or cooked. Bunches of celery should be wrapped in plastic and stored in the refrigerator. Remove any stringy fibres on the outside of celery sticks with a vegetable (potato) peeler.

Tip

Make sure there is enough sauce in the potjie as dumplings will soak up some of the liquid.

VENISON POTJIE

SERVES 6–8

45 ml (3 tbsp) olive oil
1 kg venison stewing cuts, 25 mm thick portions
3 onions, coarsely chopped
4 cloves garlic, crushed
4 sticks celery, cut into 30 mm long pieces
200 ml (¾ cup) dry red wine
160 ml (⅔ cup) strong beef stock
15 ml (1 tbsp) chopped fresh thyme
or 5 ml (1 tsp) dried
salt and freshly ground black pepper to taste
8 medium carrots, cut in half
5 medium potatoes, peeled and quartered

1. Place a cast-iron pot (No. 2) over moderate coals.
2. Heat oil and brown meat.
3. Add onions, garlic and celery and sauté until soft.
4. Add wine, stock, thyme and seasoning. Cover with lid and simmer over low coals for 2 hours.
5. Top with carrots and potatoes and simmer for another 40 minutes.

Tip
When browning meat, make sure the oil in the pot is very hot so that meat browns quickly. This seals in the flavour and gives meat a good colour.

Tomato Lamb with Dumplings (see page 78).

FROM LEFT TO RIGHT: *Sweet Potato with Rosemary, Eisbein with Dried Fruit (see page 81).*

80 on the coals

SWEET POTATO WITH ROSEMARY

This combination of sweet potato, rosemary and garlic is simply delicious.

SERVES 4–6

30 ml (2 tbsp) olive oil
30 ml (2 tbsp) butter
6 cloves garlic, peeled and sliced
80 ml (⅓ cup) vegetable stock
5 ml (1 tsp) salt
15 ml (1 tbsp) finely chopped fresh rosemary
or 5 ml (1 tsp) dried
3 medium sweet potatoes, unpeeled

1. Place a small cast-iron pot over moderate coals. Heat oil and butter and sauté garlic until soft. Add vegetable stock with salt and rosemary.
2. Cut sweet potatoes into 1 cm thick slices and place in the pot.
3. Cover with lid and simmer over moderate-low coals for 30–40 minutes until sweet potatoes are soft.

EISBEIN WITH DRIED FRUIT

SERVES 6–8

15 ml (1 tbsp) olive oil
2 medium leeks, sliced
2 smoked eisbeins (± 850 g each)
375 ml (1½ cups) apricot juice
125 ml (½ cup) meat stock
60 ml (¼ cup) medium cream sherry
salt and freshly ground black pepper to taste
125 g dried apricots
125 g sultanas

1. Place a cast-iron pot (No. 2) over moderate coals.
2. Heat oil and sauté leeks until soft.
3. Add eisbeins and brown.
4. Add apricot juice, stock, sherry and seasoning, cover with lid and simmer for about 1½ hours.
5. Add dried fruit, replace lid and simmer for another 30 minutes.

VENISON LEG IN RED WINE

SERVES 6–8

1 leg of venison (± 2.5 kg)
100 g spek (fat), cut into 10 mm strips
30 ml (2 tbsp) olive oil
salt and freshly ground black pepper to taste
5 potatoes, peeled and quartered
6 carrots, cut into 20 mm thick pieces
6 patty pans, halved
15 ml (1 tbsp) cake flour

MARINADE

80 ml (⅓ cup) olive oil
80 ml (⅓ cup) red wine vinegar
250 ml (1 cup) dry red wine
200 ml (¾ cup) strong beef stock
1 large onion, sliced
3 cloves garlic, crushed
12 peppercorns
2 bay leaves

1. Lard venison using a larding needle or by cutting incisions with a knife and stuffing them with spek.
2. For marinade: Mix all ingredients together. Place leg in marinade in refrigerator for 2–3 days. Remove meat from marinade, strain marinade and set aside.
3. Heat a cast-iron pot (No. 4) over moderate coals. Heat oil and brown meat well on all sides.
4. Add half of the marinade, a little water and seasoning, and simmer over low coals for 2½ hours.
5. Add vegetables and simmer for another 30 minutes until vegetables are soft.
6. Remove meat to carve and serve. If necessary, mix flour with a little water and use to thicken sauce.

Larding

Venison is a dry meat with very little natural fat. It therefore needs to be larded before cooking to moisten it. Traditionally, this is done with a larding needle, against the grain of the meat. If a larding needle is not available, Cut strips of pork fat or bacon and freeze. Make holes in the roast with a thin-bladed knife. Push a frozen piece of fat into each hole. Garlic can also be inserted in this way.

SEAFOOD POT WITH RICE

SERVES 6–8

30 ml (2 tbsp) olive oil
30 ml (2 tbsp) butter
2 onions, sliced
2 cloves garlic, crushed
2 green peppers, seeded and sliced
250 g calamari rings
1 kg fish fillets, cut into portions
(kabeljou, monkfish, etc.)
2 tomatoes, chopped
250 g button mushrooms, sliced
500 ml (2 cups) meat or vegetable stock
125 ml (½ cup) dry white wine
30 ml (2 tbsp) chopped fresh dill
or 10 ml (2 tsp) dried
salt and freshly ground black pepper to taste
400 g (2 cups) brown or white rice
400 g can mussels, drained

1. Place a cast-iron pot (No. 3) over moderate coals.
2. Heat oil and butter and sauté onion, garlic and peppers until soft.
3. Add calamari rings and fish and fry until golden-brown. Add tomatoes, mushrooms, stock, wine, herbs and seasoning.
4. Sprinkle rice on top of fish.
5. Cover and simmer for 45 minutes or until rice is cooked. Top with mussels 10 minutes before serving.

Tip
To prevent onions from causing tears,
chill prior to chopping.

CHICKEN CURRY

SERVES 6–8

30 ml (2 tbsp) olive oil
1.2 kg thighs, drumsticks, breasts (± 12 chicken pieces)
3 medium onions, coarsely chopped
2 cloves garlic, crushed
2 green peppers, seeded and cut into strips
15 ml (1 tbsp) finely grated root ginger
15 ml (1 tbsp) medium curry powder
400 g can tomatoes
5 ml (1 tsp) ground paprika
2 ml (¼ tsp) ground cinnamon
250 ml (1 cup) coconut milk
10 ml (2 tsp) chopped coriander leaves
salt and freshly ground black pepper to taste
250 g button mushrooms
20 ml (4 tsp) cake flour

1. Place a flat-based cast-iron pot (No. 10) over moderate coals.
2. Heat oil and brown chicken.
3. Add onions and sauté until soft. Add garlic and green pepper and stir for a few minutes until soft.
4. Add all remaining ingredients, except mushrooms and flour, and simmer over low coals for 45 minutes.
5. Add mushrooms and simmer for a further 30 minutes. Add water to flour and use to thicken sauce.

Coriander
This aromatic plant is related to parsley and the leaves
can be used fresh or dried in curry dishes. It is referred
to as *dhania* in India.

FROM TOP TO BOTTOM: *Chicken Curry, Seafood Pot with Rice (see page 82).*

potjie 83

FROM TOP TO BOTTOM: *Lamb and Pumpkin Pot, Ostrich Potjie with Sweet Potatoes (see page 85).*

84 on the coals

CURRY OFFAL

SERVES 6–8

800 g beef tripe
600 g pork trotters, sliced
30 ml (2 tbsp) olive oil
1 onion, coarsely chopped
2 cloves garlic, crushed
30 ml (2 tbsp) medium curry powder
4 tomatoes, chopped
4 potatoes, peeled and sliced

SAUCE

375 ml (1½ cups) beef stock
3 ml (½ tsp) sugar
45 ml (3 tbsp) fruit chutney
salt and freshly ground black pepper to taste

1. Rinse tripe and trotters thoroughly in salt water. Place a cast-iron pot (No. 3) over moderate coals and bring salted water to the boil. Simmer for 4 hours until soft. Remove and drain water. Cut tripe into smaller cubes.
2. Replace pot over medium heat, heat oil and sauté onion and garlic until soft. Add curry powder and stir for a minute. Add offal and top with tomatoes and potatoes.
3. For sauce: Mix all ingredients and pour over meat. Simmer for 30–45 minutes.

LAMB AND PUMPKIN POT

SERVES 6–8

1 kg lamb neck or shank slices
45 ml (3 tbsp) olive oil
2 onions, sliced
2 cloves garlic, crushed
2 green peppers, seeded and sliced
375 ml (1½ cups) meat stock
2 cinnamon sticks
15 ml (1 tbsp) chopped fresh rosemary
or 5 ml (1 tsp) dried
salt and freshly ground black pepper to taste
6 potatoes, peeled and quartered
300 g pumpkin or butternut, cut and cubed

1. Place a cast-iron pot (No. 3) over moderate coals.
2. Brown half the meat in olive oil. Remove and brown remaining meat. Then add the first batch of browned meat.
3. Add onions, garlic and green pepper and sauté until soft. Add stock, cinnamon, rosemary and seasoning.
4. Cover with lid and simmer over low coals for about 1½ hours.
5. Layer potatoes and pumpkin, replace lid and simmer for a further 30 minutes.

OSTRICH POTJIE WITH SWEET POTATOES

SERVES 6–8

45 ml (3 tbsp) olive oil
800 g ostrich neck slices, 20 mm thick
2 onions, chopped
3 cloves garlic, crushed
3 tomatoes, peeled and coarsely chopped
375 ml (1½ cups) strong meat stock
125 ml (½ cup) dry red wine
salt and freshly ground black pepper to taste
10 ml (2 tsp) chopped fresh rosemary
or 3 ml (½ tsp) dried
15 ml (1 tbsp) brown sugar
350 g green beans
3 medium sweet potatoes, sliced

1. Place a cast-iron pot (No. 2) over moderate coals.
2. Heat oil in potjie and brown meat.
3. Add onions and garlic and sauté until soft.
4. Add tomatoes, stock, wine, seasoning, herbs and sugar. Cover and simmer over low coals for about 2 hours.
5. Add beans and sweet potatoes and simmer for a further 30 minutes until soft.

spit-roast

Having a roast on the spit has always been great for special occasions and when entertaining large numbers of people. It is, however, advisable to have some knowledge and the correct equipment in order to complete this successfully. If your braai cannot accommodate a spit attachment, spit-roasting equipment can be hired for the occasion.

Meat is skewered onto the spit rod and held in place on either side with two adjustable spit forks. The rod is suspended over the heat and the food then rotates slowly, powered by either a battery or electrically driven motor.

A lamb carcass is the most popular. Smaller prime cuts of meat (such as deboned rib rolls, beef fillet or leg sections) can also be successful. The skewered meat must be evenly balanced.

Carcass

The meat choice is important. It should be from a young animal as this will result in tastier, juicier meat.

Make sure that the carcass has been well matured beforehand to improve the texture and flavour of the meat. Lamb: 2–5 days; mutton: 5–7 days; beef: 7–10 days. A carcass weighing 10 kg feeds 30 people, 15 kg feeds 40 people and 20 kg feeds 50 people.

Methods of spit-roasting

This can be done on a rotisserie or by an Argentinian method using a cross spit.

ARGENTINIAN METHOD (KNOWN AS *ASADO*)

The carcass is split open and placed on an iron rod cross to which the legs are attached. The spit is made from a piece of flat iron ± 20 mm wide and 7 mm thick. The long bar should be ± 1.7 m long and the short crossbar should be ± 0.7 m long. The spit is planted into the ground and the meat is placed on it and tilted at an angle of 45 degrees. The inner side of the carcass should face the coals. Turn the carcass halfway through to grill the other side.

HORIZONTAL METHOD

There are two methods to follow. Use an iron rod slightly longer than the carcass with two cross bars welded onto it, one at either end. The carcass is splayed out and the front and hind legs are attached to the crossbars.

The second method is to simply push the spit through the carcass (keeping the carcass whole). This is normally done when spit-roasting at home.

FOR A HOME SPIT (HORIZONTAL METHOD)

Lay the lamb flat and push the spit through the carcass, starting at the tail end. Secure the spit through the spine with string or thin wire. Season the carcass: use 5 ml (1 tsp) salt and a pinch of freshly ground black pepper per kilogram. Rub a quarter of this mixture on the inside of the stomach cavity, then use the remaining mix on the outside of the carcass, rubbing it all over towards the end of the cooking time.

A bed of moderate coals is required, which should stretch from one end of the carcass to the other. The coals must be distributed so that heat is concentrated on the thicker sections. It is recommended to have an additional fire going on the side to produce coals for the spit. Roast gradually, starting high at about 1 m and lowering to about 70 cm if required. If some sections start to burn, cover them with foil. The centre sections will braai first, whereas the legs and back will take longer.

Use a sharp knife to cut incisions in the thicker sections to speed up cooking time. This will also allow the basting to maintain moisture in the meat. Lamb should be roasted on its side for the thickest section to be closest to the coals. Thereafter concentrate on the inside rib section. The ribs protect the meat and can cope with more heat. The back section should be spit-roasted last.

RIGHT: *Lamb on the Spit (Horizontal method)*

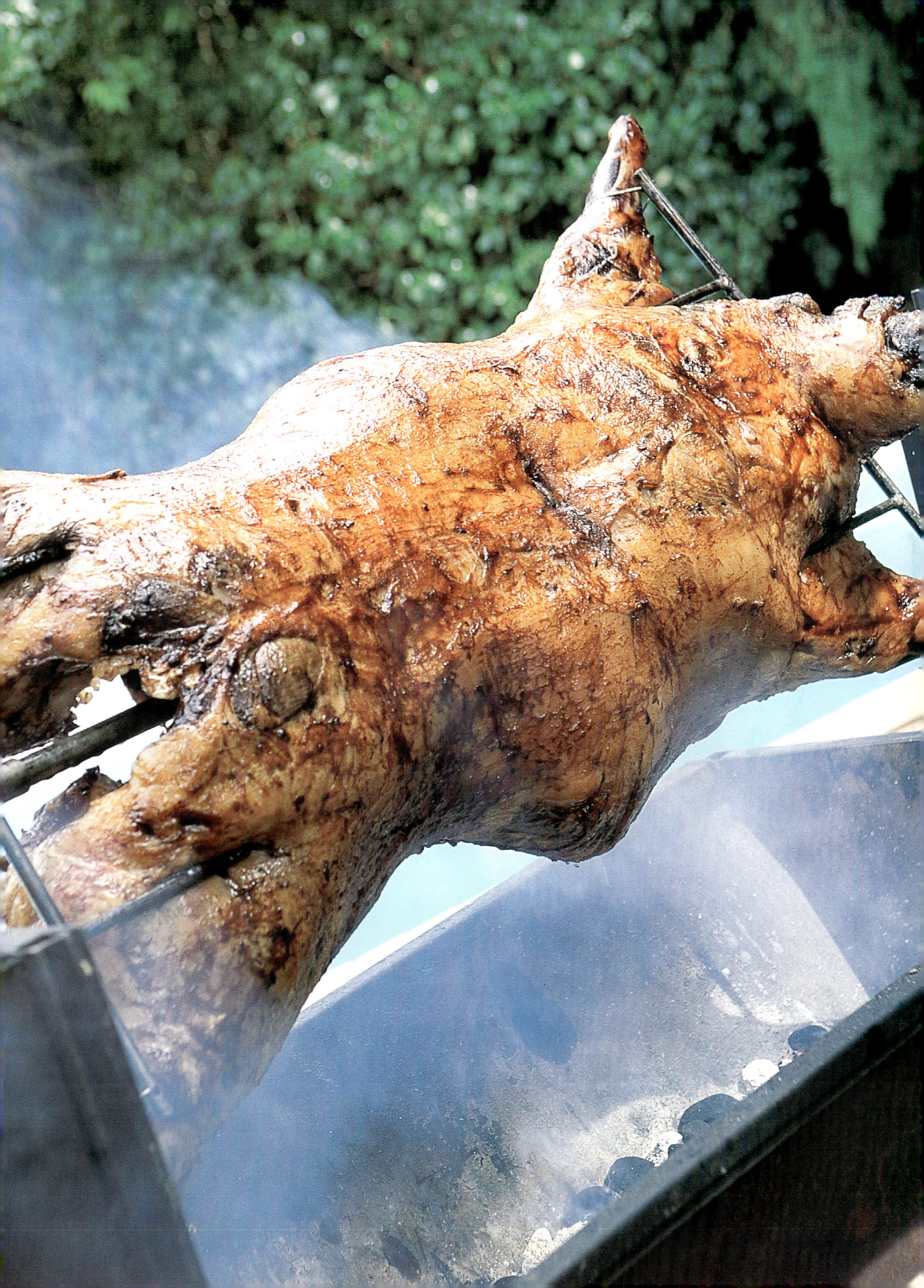

Checking for readiness

A few factors will determine the length of roasting: the size of the carcass, heat of the coals, consistency of heat and weather (if protected against wind, etc.).

As a guideline:

10 kg lamb (± 2 hours); 15 kg (± 3½ hours); 18 kg (± 5 hours). You can also use a meat thermometer to test for readiness:

Medium-done: 65 °C (150 °F)
Well-done: 70 °C (160 °F)

Carving can be done on the spit, where each person cuts off the portion of choice, or the lamb can be carved by placing it on a flat surface. Leave the meat to rest for about 10 minutes before starting to carve. Remove from the spit, open belly and remove stuffing (if used).

Use a sharp knife and start by cutting the larger cuts, such as legs and shoulders, slicing thinly against the grain.

Basting

Basting sauces are recommended for spit-roasting as they add flavour and keep the meat moist. Use any of the bastes on page 22, taking care when using those containing sweet ingredients, such as honey or sugar, as they can burn easily. Basting should only be done during the last 30 minutes of roasting.

BEEF RIB ROLL

SERVES 8–10

prime rib roll (± 2 kg)
WINE BASTE (see page 22)

1. Debone meat by cutting it away from bone. Roll tightly and secure with string along the entire length at 30 mm intervals.
2. Secure roll on rotisserie by pushing rod through roll.
3. Place over moderate coals for about 2½ hours until golden-brown.
4. For basting sauce: Double-up recipe. Brush meat frequently during the last 30 minutes.
5. Remove from spit and rest meat for 10 minutes before carving.

PAPRIKA CHICKEN

SERVES 4–6

1 whole chicken (± 1.2 kg)
BASTING SAUCE
50 g butter, melted
30 ml (2 tbsp) olive oil
30 ml (2 tbsp) fresh lemon juice
15 ml (1 tbsp) ground paprika
3 ml (½ tsp) cayenne pepper
2 cloves garlic, crushed
salt and freshly ground black pepper to taste

1. Truss chicken to ensure that its shape is maintained.
2. Secure chicken on rotisserie by pushing rod through bird from tail to front.
3. Cook over moderate coals for about 1¼ hours until cooked through.
4. For basting sauce: Mix all ingredients together and baste chicken frequently during the last 30 minutes.

> ### Trussing
> It is necessary to truss a chicken to keep its shape and to allow for even cooking.

THYME STUFFING

FOR 1 CHICKEN

50 g (± 3 rashers) bacon, finely chopped
100 g chicken livers, finely chopped
375 ml (1½ cups) freshly prepared brown or white breadcrumbs
45 ml (3 tbsp) milk
5 ml (1 tsp) sugar
80 ml (⅓ cup) chopped fresh thyme or 30 ml (2 tbsp) dried
15 ml (1 tbsp) chopped fresh parsley or 5 ml (1 tsp) dried
2 ml (¼ tsp) salt
freshly ground black pepper to taste

1. Mix all ingredients together and spoon the stuffing into the chicken cavity.

Pork Neck Roll

PORK NECK ROLL

SERVES 6–8

pork neck roll (± 1.2 kg)
BASTING SAUCE
125 ml (½ cup) fresh lemon juice
80 ml (⅓ cup) olive oil
60 ml (¼ cup) medium cream sherry
15 ml (1 tbsp) soya sauce
45 ml (3 tbsp) light brown sugar
15 ml (1 tbsp) finely chopped root ginger
2 cloves garlic, crushed
salt and freshly ground black pepper to taste

1. Debone pork, then roll tightly and secure with string along the entire length at 30 mm intervals.
2. Secure roll on rotisserie by pushing rod through roll.
3. Roast over moderate coals for about 2¼ hours until cooked through.
4. For basting sauce: Mix all ingredients together and baste pork roll during the last 30 minutes.
5. Remove from spit and rest meat for 10 minutes before carving.

accompaniments

breads

FRUIT HEALTH BREAD

*This home-made bread is a favourite amongst guests.
Small individual loaves can also be baked.*

MAKES 1 LOAF

250 ml (1 cup) crushed wheat
500 ml (2 cups) whole-wheat flour
250 ml (1 cup) digestive bran
250 ml (1 cup) rolled oats
10 ml (2 tsp) baking powder
7 ml (1¼ tsp) salt
7 ml (1¼ tsp) bicarbonate of soda
45 ml (3 tbsp) light brown sugar
125 ml (½ cup) fruit cake mix
500 ml (2 cups) buttermilk
60 ml (¼ cup) milk

1. Preheat oven to 180 °C (350 °F).
2. Mix all the dry ingredients and fruit cake mix.
3. Add buttermilk. Add milk to empty buttermilk container, shake and add to mixture. Mix thoroughly.
4. Spoon into a greased 23 cm loaf tin.
5. Bake for 50–60 minutes. Allow to cool before serving sliced and buttered.

Bran
Bran is an excellent source of fibre, which is essential for a healthy digestive system.

MEDITERRANEAN PIZZA

SERVES 4–6

DOUGH
As per Roosterkoek (see page 93)

TOPPING
410 g can tomato and onion mix
6 cloves garlic, chopped
50 g (¼ cup) chopped spinach, cooked
8 black olives, pitted
15 ml (1 tbsp) chopped fresh mixed herbs
or 5 ml (1 tsp) dried
salt and freshly ground black pepper to taste
200 g Feta cheese, crumbled slightly
150 g Mozzarella cheese, grated
15 ml (1 tbsp) olive oil

1. Prepare dough as per the method on page 93.
2. When dough has doubled in size, knead it down and roll it out into four pizza bases of about 20 cm in diameter, or smaller individual ones if preferred. Dust with flour.
3. Cook the pizza dough for the base over low coals for 3–5 minutes, until the dough is lightly browned underneath. Turn pizza base over, so that the cooked side is uppermost.
4. Spread the pizza with the tomato and onion mix, then sprinkle with the chopped garlic. Top with spinach, olives and herbs. Season. Sprinkle feta and mozzarella on top, then drizzle with olive oil.
5. Cook until the topping has melted and the dough has puffed up and turned golden-brown, about 12–15 minutes.

RIGHT: *Mediterranean Pizza*

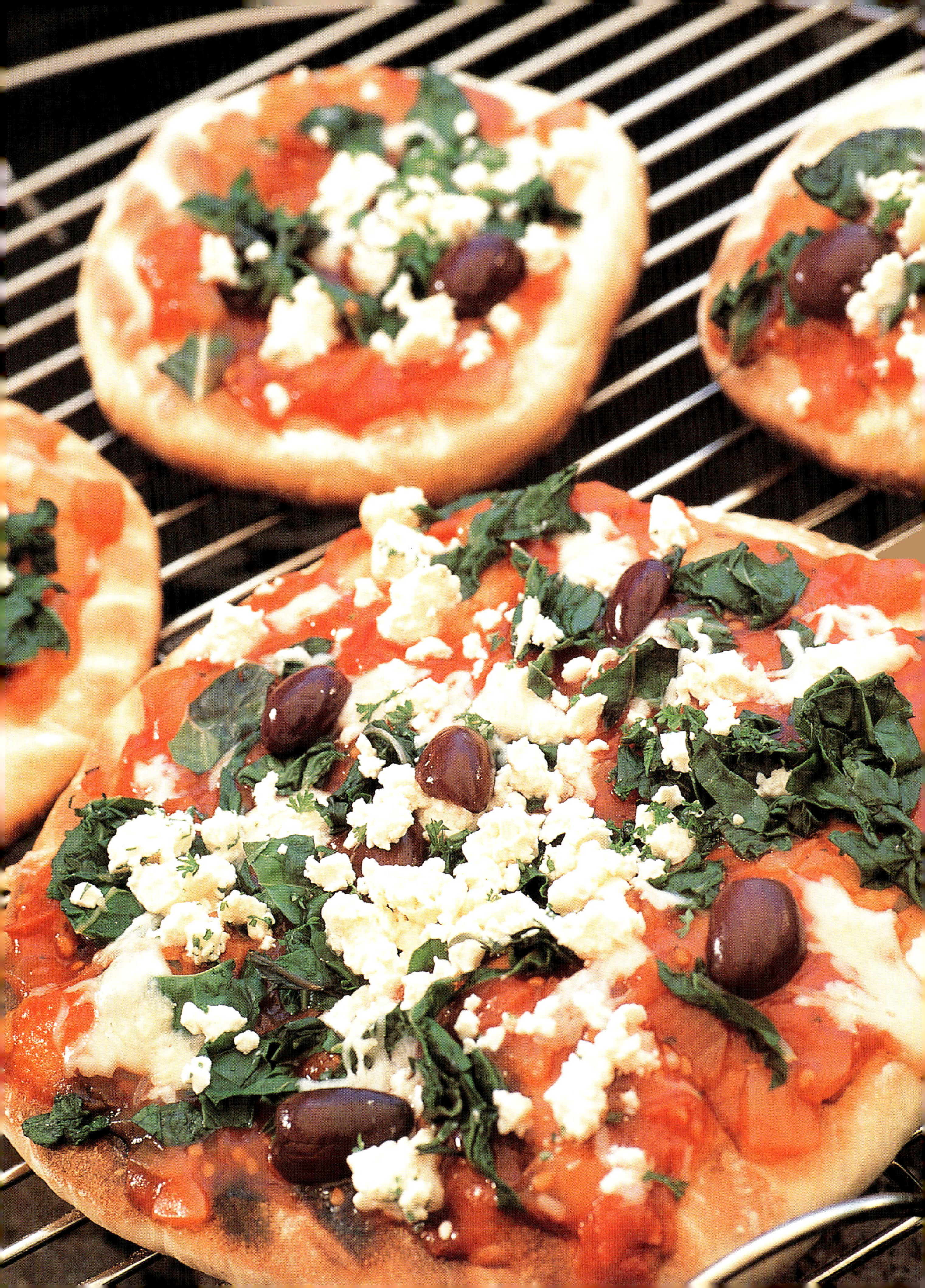

CHEESE AND SUN-DRIED TOMATO BREAD

SERVES 5–6

30 g sun-dried tomatoes
15 ml (1 tbsp) butter
1 medium onion, chopped
2 cloves garlic, crushed
10 ml (2 tsp) sugar
500 ml (2 cups) buttermilk
3 eggs, beaten
850 ml (3½ cups) self-raising flour
5 ml (1 tsp) salt
2 ml (¼ tsp) cayenne pepper
5 ml (1 tsp) chopped fresh parsley or 2 ml (¼ tsp) dried
5 ml (1 tsp) chopped fresh origanum or basil
or 2 ml (¼ tsp) dried
50 g (½ cup) grated Cheddar cheese

1. Preheat oven to 180 °C (350 °F).
2. Pour boiling water over sun-dried tomatoes and soak for about 30 minutes. Drain and chop coarsely.
3. Heat butter in a heavy-based saucepan. Sauté onion and garlic until soft. Remove from heat and transfer to a large bowl. Add sun-dried tomatoes and sugar.
4. Beat buttermilk and eggs together and set aside.
5. Sift flour, salt and cayenne pepper, then add herbs. Mix flour and egg mixture into onion mix until well combined. Fold in cheese. Add more milk if needed.
6. Spoon mixture into a greased 23 cm loaf tin and bake for 50–60 minutes. Serve with butter.

FROM LEFT TO RIGHT: *Askoek, Roosterkoek (see page 93), Cheese and Sun-dried Tomato Bread.*

ROOSTERKOEK

This basic dough made with yeast is very versatile.

MAKES 20–24

1 kg (7 cups) cake flour
7 ml (1¼ tsp) sugar
2 ml (¼ tsp) salt
10 g (3 tsp) instant dry yeast
± 600 ml lukewarm water
15 ml (1 tbsp) butter, melted

1. Sift flour, sugar and salt together. Add yeast.
2. Add enough lukewarm water to mix to a stiff dough. Knead dough for about 5 minutes until smooth and not sticky.
3. Brush melted butter over the dough. Cover and leave in a warm place to double in size. Knead down and shape into balls. Press down slightly and sprinkle with a little flour.
4. Cook over low coals for 50–60 minutes until done, then serve hot with butter.

ASKOEK

MAKES ABOUT 16

1. Use recipe as above. Continue from step 3. Make balls slightly bigger. Place in warm ash (burned out coals) for 30–45 minutes until done. Remove cooked rolls from ash, knock off excess ash and serve hot with butter.

STOKBROOD

MAKES ABOUT 12

1. Use recipe as above. Continue from step 3. Roll pieces of dough to a length of about 20 cm. Wind dough around skewers and braai over low coals until done. Remove sticks and fill hollows with butter and syrup.

MEALIE BREAD

MAKES 1 LOAF

375 ml (1½ cups) cake flour
250 ml (1 cup) maize meal
15 ml (1 tbsp) baking powder
2 ml (¼ tsp) salt
125 ml (½ cup) sugar
125 ml (½ cup) cooking oil
3 eggs, beaten
410 g can creamed sweetcorn

1. Preheat oven to 180 °C (350 °F).
2. Sift cake flour, maize meal, baking powder and salt together. Add all remaining ingredients and mix well.
3. Spoon mixture into a greased 23 cm loaf tin and bake for 50–60 minutes. Serve warm with butter.

SAVOURY BUTTERS

Mix butter by hand or in food processor with the desired flavouring, shape into a roll on foil and chill in the freezer for a short while to set.

Herb
125 g softened butter, 30 ml (2 tbsp) chopped fresh herbs (parsley, thyme and dill)

Lemon-garlic
125 g softened butter, 4 cloves garlic, crushed and 15 ml (1 tbsp) fresh lemon juice

Parmesan and mustard
125 g softened butter, 30 ml (2 tbsp) finely grated Parmesan cheese and 10 ml (2 tsp) whole-grain mustard

Black pepper
125 g softened butter and 15 ml (1 tbsp) ground black pepper

Sun-dried tomato and basil
125 g softened butter, 12 g sun-dried tomatoes, soaked and chopped; 5 ml (1 tsp) sugar; 2 cloves garlic, crushed and 15 ml (1 tbsp) chopped fresh basil or 5 ml (1 tsp) dried

STIFF MEALIE MEAL PORRIDGE (STYWE PAP)

This porridge is ideal to serve with barbecue sauce (see page 35) at a braai. Warm any left-overs and serve with milk and sugar for breakfast.

SERVES 6

1 litre (4 cups) water
10 ml (2 tsp) salt
20 ml (4 tsp) butter
750 ml (3 cups) mealie meal

1. Bring water to the boil in a heavy-based saucepan, then add salt, butter and mealie meal to water. Do not stir.
2. Reduce heat to very low, cover and simmer for 10–15 minutes. Stir with a cutting movement to mix the mealie meal into the water. Replace lid and simmer further for approximately 45 minutes.

CRUMBLY MEALIE MEAL PORRIDGE (KRUMMELPAP)

Serve at a braai with tomato sauce, or with milk and sugar for breakfast.

SERVES 6

750 ml (3 cups) water
10 ml (2 tsp) salt
1 litre (4 cups) mealie meal
410 g can kernel corn (optional)

1. Bring water to the boil in a heavy-based saucepan. Add salt and then slowly add mealie meal so that it piles up in the centre, with the water boiling round it. Do not stir.
2. Reduce heat, cover and simmer for 10–15 minutes. Stir with a fork until mixture is crumbly. Continue cooking over low heat for 20–30 minutes, then stir in kernel corn, if preferred. The porridge should be crumbly.

SAVOURY PAP TART

SERVES 6–8

1 litre (4 cups) water
250 ml (1 cup) mealie meal
3 ml (½ tsp) salt
15 ml (1 tbsp) cooking oil
1 onion, finely chopped
250 g rindless streaky bacon, chopped
250 g button mushrooms, sliced
3 tomatoes, finely chopped
salt and freshly ground black pepper to taste
60 ml (¼ cup) fresh cream (optional)
100 g (1 cup) grated Cheddar cheese

1. Preheat oven to 180 °C (350 °F).
2. Bring water to the boil in a heavy-based saucepan. Add mealie meal and salt and stir thoroughly. Simmer for about 12 minutes until cooked, stirring occasionally.
3. Heat oil in a large, heavy-based pan. Sauté onion and bacon until soft.
4. Add mushrooms, tomatoes and seasoning and leave to simmer for about 10 minutes until most of the liquid has evaporated.
5. Add cream if using. Spoon alternate layers of pap and onion mixture into a large ovenproof dish. Top with grated cheese and bake for about 20 minutes.

TOAST BREADS

MAKES 4

8 slices white bread, 1 cm thick
50 g butter
100 g (1 cup) grated Cheddar cheese
1 medium tomato, sliced
1 medium onion, sliced

1. Butter one side of each slice.
2. Top with cheese, tomato and onion as preferred, then top with another slice of bread.
3. Braai over low coals for 5–8 minutes in total until cheese has melted.

CLOCKWISE FROM TOP LEFT: *Honey Potbrood, Mealie Bread, Savoury Butters – Sundried Tomato and Basil, Black Pepper, Parmesan and Mustard, Herb (see page 93).*

HONEY POTBROOD

SERVES 6–8

250 ml (1 cup) whole-wheat flour
850 g (6 cups) white bread flour
5 ml (1 tsp) salt
10 g (3 tsp) instant dry yeast
7 ml (1¼ tsp) sugar
20 ml (4 tsp) cooking oil
30 ml (2 tbsp) honey
± 600 ml luke-warm water

1. Sift flours and salt into a bowl, adding any bran left over in the sieve.
2. Sprinkle yeast and sugar over flour mixture.
3. Stir oil and honey into half of the water. Add with remaining water to flour and mix to a soft dough. Turn out dough onto a floured surface and knead until smooth. Cover and leave in a warm place until double in size. Knead down.
4. Place dough in a well-greased cast-iron pot (No. 12), dust with flour on top and leave to rise. Place pot over moderate coals for about 1 hour. Turn bread out and tap underneath. If it sounds hollow, it is ready.

Tip
Place a few low coals on top of the lid towards the end of the cooking time. This will ensure that the bread browns and does not stay soggy on top. Alternatively, turn the bread in the pot after 45 minutes.

accompaniments

vegetables

CHAR-GRILLED VEGETABLES
A healthy way of serving an assortment of vegetables.

SERVES 4–6

4 slices pumpkin or butternut
3 medium onions
2 red or green peppers
1 large aubergine (brinjal)
4 baby marrows
2 large tomatoes

BASTING SAUCE
125 ml (½ cup) olive oil
60 ml (¼ cup) fresh lemon juice
3 ml (½ tsp) light soya sauce
2 ml (¼ tsp) Worcestershire sauce
1 clove garlic, crushed

1. To prepare vegetables: Cut pumpkin slices into 10 mm thick cubes. Peel and halve the onions. Cut peppers in half, remove seeds and cut in half again. Cut aubergine lengthwise into 10 mm thick slices. Top and tail the baby marrows, and cut the tomatoes in half.
2. For basting sauce: Mix all ingredients together.
3. Braai vegetables over moderate coals for 30–35 minutes, basting frequently with sauce until vegetables start to turn golden-brown.

Variation
VEGETABLE KEBABS
Blanch vegetables for 1 minute in microwave at 100% power to soften slightly. This enables easier threading on skewers. Use a variety of colourful vegetables, such as aubergine (brinjal), red or green pepper, onion, baby marrow, mushrooms and cherry tomatoes. Grill for about 20 minutes, basting frequently with above basting sauce.

VEGETABLE PARCELS IN FOIL
Great as a side dish or for vegetarians. An endless variety of vegetables can be used.

SERVES 4–6

1 butternut, seeds removed and cut into 10 mm thick slices
4 medium potatoes, peeled and cut into 10 mm thick slices
2 sweet potatoes, cut into 10 mm thick slices
1 aubergine (brinjal), cut into 10 mm thick slices
125 g button mushrooms, sliced
1 tomato, sliced
2 onions, sliced
salt and freshly ground black pepper to taste
± 50 g herb or lemon-garlic butter (see page 93)
45 ml (3 tbsp) honey

1. Cut foil into 40 x 40 cm squares, then fold them in half to make a double layer.
2. Place a variety of the above vegetables in the centre of each piece of foil (shiny side facing inwards).
3. Season. Place about 5 ml (1 tsp) herb or garlic butter and about 5 ml (1 tsp) of honey over each. Bring up opposite foil edges and seal, folding double. Fold in remaining edges to close, leaving a little space for steam to build up.
4. Place parcels on a grid over moderate coals for 45–50 minutes, depending on size of parcels.

Aubergine
Also known as brinjal or eggplant. Work quickly when cutting, as it will discolour fast. To draw out the bitter taste, sprinkle with salt and leave for about 30 minutes. Pat dry with paper towel.

SWEET POTATO IN COALS

Place unpeeled sweet potatoes in warm ash, covering completely. Leave for about 40 minutes until soft.

FROM TOP TO BOTTOM: *Vegetable Parcels in Foil, Char-grilled Vegetables (see page 96).*

accompaniments 97

Stuffed Pumpkin (see page 99).

EASY POTATOES WITH SOUP POWDER

SERVES 4–6

8 medium potatoes
125 g butter
90 g (1 pkt) white or brown onion soup powder

1. Preheat oven to 180 °C (350 °F).
2. Wash potatoes and dry with paper towel. Make vertical cuts 10 mm apart through potatoes, almost to the base. Place in an ovenproof dish.
3. Melt butter, without boiling. Add soup powder and pour over potatoes.
4. Bake for 1¼ hours, basting frequently.

JACKET POTATOES WITH SOUR CREAM AND CHIVES

6 medium potatoes
125 ml (½ cup) sour cream
15 ml (1 tbsp) chopped fresh chives or 5 ml (1 tsp) dried
salt and freshly ground black pepper to taste

1. Wash potatoes and dry with paper towel.
2. Wrap each potato in foil, shiny side facing inwards. Place in moderate coals for about 30 minutes until soft. Alternatively, place in preheated oven of 180 °C (350 °F) for about 1 hour.
3. Mix sour cream, chives and seasoning. Cut a cross in the top of each potato and spoon on sour cream.

Variation
Lemon-garlic butter (see page 93) can be substituted for the sour cream.

POTATO AND MUSHROOM BAKE

Deliciously creamy – ideal for the winter menu.

SERVES 4

8 medium potatoes, peeled
30 ml (2 tbsp) cooking oil
1 onion, coarsely chopped
250 g button mushrooms, halved
2 cloves garlic, crushed
10 ml (2 tsp) chopped fresh origanum
or 3 ml (½ tsp) dried
salt and freshly ground black pepper to taste
250 ml (1 cup) fresh cream

1. Preheat oven to 180 °C (350 °F).
2. Cook potatoes until soft, then cut into slices. Place in an oven-proof dish.
3. Heat oil and fry onion until soft. Add mushrooms and fry until slightly soft. Remove from heat and spread over potatoes. Sprinkle over origanum and seasoning.
4. Pour cream over and bake for about 45 minutes.

Variation
Substitute the mushrooms with 125 g bacon, chopped and fried.

CORN ON THE COB

4 whole corn on the cob, husks and silk removed

1. Break or cut each cob into 3 pieces.
2. Place on a grid over moderate-low coals for 20–30 minutes. Remove from heat and spread with butter.

Variation
Use the basting sauce from char-grilled vegetables (see page 96) for a delicious flavour and to add colour to corn.

STUFFED PUMPKIN

SERVES 8

1 medium pumpkin, about 20 cm in diameter
FILLING
250 g rindless streaky bacon, chopped
250 ml (1 cup) freshly prepared brown
or white breadcrumbs
125 ml (½ cup) grated Parmesan cheese
30 ml (2 tbsp) chopped fresh parsley
or 15 ml (1 tbsp) dried
5 ml (1 tsp) chopped fresh origanum or 2 ml (¼ tsp) dried
salt and freshly ground black pepper to taste
30 ml (2 tbsp) olive oil
80 ml (⅓ cup) fresh cream

1. Preheat oven to 180 °C (350 °F).
2. Cut a round piece off the top of the pumpkin, and remove all the pips from inside.
3. For filling: Fry bacon in heavy-based saucepan until soft. Remove from heat and stir in remaining ingredients, except olive oil. Fill pumpkin with mixture, then drizzle with olive oil.
4. Cover with 'pumpkin lid'. Place in a flat, greased cast-iron pot (No. 12), cover with lid and bake in oven for 1½–2 hours.

GARLIC OVER COALS

Fresh garlic in bulbs (whole head, unpeeled)

1. Place whole garlic bulbs on grill. Cook over low coals for about 25 minutes until flesh is soft and creamy.
2. Separate the cloves and use a sharp knife to scoop out the flesh of individual cloves. Chop or mash into a purée and spread on bread or meat.

Tip
Garlic purée can be added to marinades, flavoured butters and soups. It will keep for up to one week in the refrigerator. Roasting garlic produces a mild flavour.

salads & dressings

SPINACH SALAD

A classic and very nutritious salad. The leaves soak up all the flavours of the dressing.

SERVES 4–6

125 g streaky bacon, chopped
1 medium onion, chopped
150 g spinach leaves, finely shredded
125 g button mushrooms, sliced
50 g (1 punnet) bean sprouts
2 eggs, hard-boiled and chopped

DRESSING

30 ml (2 tbsp) wine vinegar
60 ml (¼ cup) tomato sauce
60 ml (¼ cup) olive oil
60 ml (¼ cup) sugar
30 ml (2 tbsp) Worcestershire sauce

1. Fry bacon in a heavy-based saucepan, without adding any fat. Fry until starting to brown then remove with slotted spoon and drain on absorbent paper. Add onion to pan and stir through until softened. Place bacon and onion in a mixing bowl and add spinach and mushrooms.
2. For dressing: Whisk all ingredients together, pour over salad and toss lightly.
3. Top with bean sprouts and chopped egg. Toss lightly again and serve.

Variation
Substitute bean sprouts with chickpeas.

Tip
Add dressing just before serving. Never add dressing too far in advance as the leaves will become soggy.

POTATO SALAD WITH HOT BACON DRESSING

SERVES 6–8

10 (± 1.5 kg) medium potatoes, unpeeled
250 g streaky bacon, chopped
1 large onion, chopped
80 ml (⅓ cup) olive oil
60 ml (¼ cup) vinegar
5 ml (1 tsp) sugar
3 ml (½ tsp) mustard powder
salt and freshly ground black pepper to taste
10 ml (2 tsp) chopped fresh parsley or 2 ml (¼ tsp) dried

1. Boil potatoes until soft, then drain and cut into 15 mm cubes.
2. Fry bacon in a heavy-based saucepan until lightly browned. Add onion and sauté until soft.
3. Add remaining ingredients, except parsley, and bring to the boil. Stir into potatoes and mix lightly. Top with parsley and serve immediately.

SWEET-AND-SOUR ONIONS

SERVES 4–6

1 kg pickling onions, peeled
3 ml (½ tsp) salt
125 ml (½ cup) sugar
125 ml (½ cup) vinegar
20 ml (4 tsp) custard powder
30 ml (2 tbsp) water

1. Peel onions and place in a heavy-based saucepan. Cover with water, add salt and boil for about 20 minutes until soft. Drain off water.
2. Add sugar and vinegar and bring to the boil.
3. Dissolve custard powder in water and stir into onions, boiling until mixture thickens. Simmer for a few minutes, then leave to cool. Can be kept in the refrigerator for up to 2 days.

100 on the coals

CLOCKWISE FROM TOP LEFT: *Fruit Health Bread (see page 90), Spinach Salad, Potato Salad with Hot Bacon Dressing (see page 100).*

accompaniments 101

THREE-BEAN SALAD WITH BASIL

Prepare in advance as it's handy to have ready.

SERVES 6

420 g can baked beans
410 g can butter beans, drained
410 g can green beans, drained
125 ml (½ cup) vinegar
125 ml (½ cup) light brown sugar
80 ml (⅓ cup) olive oil
1 onion, chopped
1 green pepper, seeded and chopped
5 ml (1 tsp) mustard powder
15 ml (1 tbsp) chopped fresh basil or 5 ml (1 tsp) dried
2 ml (¼ tsp) salt

1. Mix the three cans of beans.
2. Add remaining ingredients and mix well. Leave for 2 hours to chill before serving. Can be kept in refrigerator for a few days. Alternatively, seal in glass jars.

MARINATED VEGETABLES

Healthier and tastier if olive oil is used instead of cooking oil.

SERVES 4–6

400 g can small artichoke hearts, drained
250 g button mushrooms, halved

MARINADE
80 ml (⅓ cup) olive oil
60 ml (¼ cup) white wine vinegar
5 ml (1 tsp) sugar
3 ml (½ tsp) salt
5 ml (1 tsp) chopped fresh dill or 2 ml (¼ tsp) dried
1 medium onion, finely chopped

1. Cut artichoke hearts in half and place in a medium-sized bowl. Add mushrooms.
2. For marinade: Mix all ingredients together and stir through vegetables. Cover and marinate in the refrigerator overnight. Stir occasionally.

CURRIED BROWN RICE AND LENTIL SALAD

A delicious lentil salad in the new-style trend.

SERVES 4–6

375 ml (1½ cups) cooked brown rice or any pasta shells
125 ml (½ cup) cooked brown lentils
1 onion, chopped
1 green pepper, seeded and chopped
410 g can peaches, drained and chopped
60 ml (¼ cup) mayonnaise
30 ml (2 tbsp) fruit chutney
15 ml (1 tbsp) medium curry powder
30 ml (2 tbsp) fresh lemon juice

1. Mix all ingredients together.
2. Leave in the refrigerator for a few hours, or chill overnight if preferred.

Variation

Add 5 ml (1 tsp) ground cumin for a spicy Middle-Eastern flavour.

Lentils

Lentils are low in fat and are available in several varieties, from green and brown to orange-red. They do not have to be soaked beforehand as they cook very quickly. Lentils keep well in a cool, dark place.

CREAMY YOGHURT DRESSING

125 ml (½ cup) mayonnaise
125 ml (½ cup) plain, unflavoured yoghurt
20 ml (4 tsp) honey
5 ml (1 tsp) chopped fresh parsley or 2 ml (¼ tsp) dried

1. Combine all ingredients and keep refrigerated.

BROCCOLI SALAD

SERVES 4–6

1 kg fresh broccoli
250 g fresh button mushrooms

MARINADE

125 ml (½ cup) sugar
250 ml (1 cup) cooking oil
60 ml (¼ cup) apple vinegar
5 ml (1 tsp) salt
1 small onion, finely chopped
5 ml (1 tsp) paprika

1. For marinade: Mix all ingredients together.
2. Cut broccoli into small florets. Wash thoroughly, drain and add mushrooms. Pour marinade over and stir through well.
3. Marinate for 2–3 hours or preferably overnight in the refrigerator. When serving, strain salad from the marinade.

PASTA SALAD WITH OLIVES AND SUN-DRIED TOMATOES

SERVES 6–8

200 g fusilli (corkscrew pasta)
30 g (±12) sun-dried tomatoes
100 g (± 12) black pitted olives
1 green pepper, seeded and finely chopped
balsamic, garlic and herb salad dressing (see this page)

1. Cook pasta until soft, then drain.
2. Pour hot water over sun-dried tomatoes. Leave for 30 minutes to soften slightly. Drain and chop coarsely. Add, with olives and green pepper, to pasta.
3. Serve with balsamic, garlic and herb dressing.

Tip
Cook pasta *al denté* – firm to the bite, not soggy.

BALSAMIC, GARLIC AND HERB DRESSING

60 ml (¼ cup) balsamic or wine vinegar
1 clove garlic, crushed
salt and freshly ground black pepper to taste
80 ml (⅓ cup) olive oil
15 ml (1 tbsp) chopped fresh origanum
or 5 ml (1 tsp) dried

1. Mix the balsamic vinegar with garlic and season to taste.
2. Gradually add olive oil, whisking all the time. Add origanum.

Balsamic vinegar
This vinegar has a rich, dark colour with a spicy, nutty flavour. It is produced from white wine grapes and matured for a few years in wooden barrels. It tastes delicious over grilled food or in sauces. Because heat influences the taste, it is best to add it at the end of the cooking time.

MUSTARD AND HONEY DRESSING

200 ml (¾ cup) olive oil
80 ml (⅓ cup) fresh lemon juice
4 cloves garlic, crushed
15 ml (1 tbsp) whole-grain mustard
30 ml (2 tbsp) honey
salt and freshly ground black pepper to taste

1. Whisk the olive oil and lemon juice until combined.
2. Add all remaining ingredients and refrigerate.

accompaniments

desserts

TIRAMISU

This increasingly popular Italian dessert is so easy to make and should be prepared at least a day in advance.

SERVES 6

250 g Mascarpone or cream cheese
3 eggs, separated
125 ml (½ cup) fresh cream, whipped
125 ml (½ cup) castor sugar
250 ml (1 cup) strong black coffee
60 ml (¼ cup) Kahlua liqueur (optional)
375 g sponge biscuits
15 ml (1 tbsp) cocoa powder to garnish

1. Combine cheese and egg yolks in a mixing bowl and beat until smooth. Fold in whipped cream.
2. In a separate bowl, add 60 ml (¼ cup) sugar to egg whites and beat until soft peak stage.
3. Fold egg whites into cheese mixture using a metal spoon.
4. Combine coffee, liqueur and remaining sugar. Use tongs to dip biscuits one at a time into coffee mixture. Be careful not to soak too long as the biscuits will become soggy and break up.
5. Layer half of the biscuits in the base of a rectangular or round dish, and top with cheese mixture. Continue layers with remaining biscuits and cheese mix. Dust with cocoa powder just before serving.

Mascarpone cheese

This soft dessert cheese is made from cream and is available from delicatessens. It can be substituted with cream cheese or smooth cottage cheese.

MALVA PUDDING

SERVES 4–6

250 ml (1 cup) milk
15 ml (1 tbsp) butter
15 ml (1 tbsp) apricot jam
15 ml (1 tbsp) vinegar
1 egg
200 ml (¾ cup) castor sugar
250 ml (1 cup) self-raising flour
5 ml (1 tsp) bicarbonate of soda

SAUCE

250 ml (1 cup) evaporated milk
100 g butter
125 ml (½ cup) sugar

1. Preheat oven to 180 °C (350 °F).
2. For pudding: Heat milk, butter and jam in a heavy-based saucepan over low heat until butter has melted. Remove from heat to cool slightly, then add vinegar.
3. Whisk egg and sugar until light and fluffy.
4. Sift flour and bicarbonate of soda and fold into egg mixture together with warm milk.
5. Pour into a deep ovenproof dish and bake for 15 minutes. Reduce heat to 160 °C (325 °F) and bake for a further 30–40 minutes.
6. For sauce: Simmer all ingredients for 3 minutes and pour sauce immediately over warm pudding when taken out of the oven.

RIGHT: *Tiramisu*

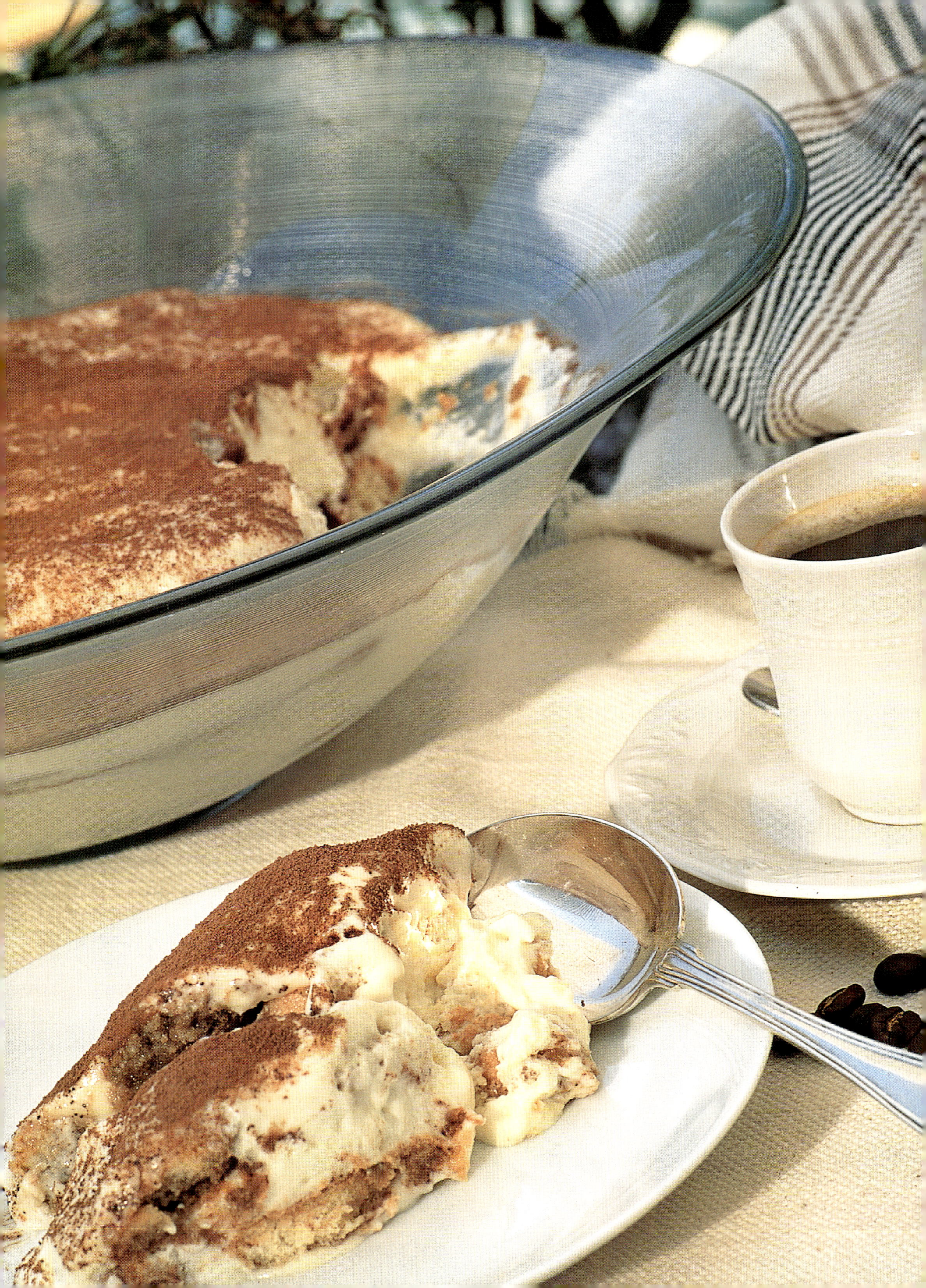

SPICY DUMPLINGS

SERVES 4

250 ml (1 cup) cake flour
2 ml (¼ tsp) salt
5 ml (1 tsp) bicarbonate of soda
15 ml (1 tbsp) butter
1 egg, beaten
30 ml (2 tbsp) milk
15 ml (1 tbsp) smooth apricot jam

SYRUP

375 ml (1½ cups) water
250 ml (1 cup) sugar
5 ml (1 tsp) ground cinnamon
5 ml (1 tsp) ground ginger
2 ml (¼ tsp) ground nutmeg

1. Sift flour, salt and bicarbonate of soda together. Rub in butter.
2. Beat egg, milk and apricot jam together. Mix into flour until combined.
3. For syrup: Mix all ingredients together and bring to the boil in a heavy-based saucepan.
4. Drop spoonfuls of dough into the boiling syrup. Cover and boil for 12–15 minutes. Do not remove the lid while cooking. Serve with custard or cream.

Variation

Add 80 ml (⅓ cup) chopped, pitted dates to flour mixture for spicy date dumplings.

MARSHMALLOWS OVER THE COALS

SERVES 6–8

120 g packet marshmallows (about 20)
wooden skewers

1. Thread about 3 marshmallows on each skewer.
2. Hold marshmallows directly over hot coals for a few minutes. The outside will start to brown and the inside will begin to melt.

BREAD AND BUTTER PUDDING

A classic pudding that always remains popular. Use dried apricots for variation, but omit for a traditional pudding.

SERVES 6–8

10–12 slices white or brown bread
60 g butter
125 g dried apricots, coarsely chopped
75 g raisins
3 eggs
125 ml (½ cup) castor sugar
250 ml (1 cup) milk
250 ml (1 cup) fresh cream
5 ml (1 tsp) lemon rind
3 ml (½ tsp) vanilla essence

1. Preheat oven to 180 °C (350 °F).
2. Remove crusts from bread, butter and cut each into four wedges.
3. Layer bread, buttered-side up, in a large greased oven-proof dish. Sprinkle apricots and raisins over.
4. Beat eggs and sugar in a bowl. Add milk, cream, lemon rind and essence and pour over bread. Leave to soak in slightly.
5. Bake for 30–40 minutes or until custard sets.

Vanilla

This pod from a type of orchid is yellow-green when picked and dark brown after curing and drying. It can be kept in a jar of castor sugar to make vanilla sugar. Vanilla essence is normally used because the pods are not always easily obtainable. Vanilla is used for flavouring sweet dishes.

GRILLED BANANAS

SERVES 4

4–6 ripe bananas, unpeeled

1. Grill bananas over moderate coals for about 20 minutes until skin becomes very black and the fruit feels soft.
2. Remove from heat, peel and serve warm.

Bread and Butter Pudding (see page 106)

FLAMBÉED BANANAS

An impressive dessert. Substitute bananas with any other fruit of choice.

SERVES 4–6

60 g butter
80 ml (⅓ cup) brown sugar
125 ml (½ cup) fresh orange juice
5 ml (1 tsp) finely grated orange rind
6 ripe bananas, peeled and sliced lengthways
2 ml (¼ tsp) ground cinnamon
80 ml (⅓ cup) brandy
30 g toasted flaked almonds (optional)

1. Heat the butter in a large frying pan or skottel. Add sugar and stir until dissolved.
2. Add the juice, rind and bananas to the pan and cook for about 3 minutes. Sprinkle cinnamon over bananas.
3. Heat brandy slightly, then pour over bananas and ignite. Allow the flames to subside.
4. Serve bananas with sauce and sprinkle with toasted flaked almonds.

Tips
- To toast almonds, place a layer on a baking tray and bake at 150 °C (300 °F), turning constantly until golden-brown.
- The alcohol, as well as the food, must be hot before it will ignite. When the alcohol has burned off, the flame dies away naturally, leaving only the essence.

SUPERB CHOCOLATE MOUSSE

SERVES 6

300 g dark chocolate
30 ml (2 tbsp) butter
3 eggs, separated
60 ml (¼ cup) castor sugar
5 ml (1 tsp) vanilla essence
30 ml (2 tbsp) brandy or Van der Hum liqueur
250 ml (1 cup) fresh cream, whipped
grated chocolate for topping

1. Break up chocolate and place in the top of a double boiler, stirring until melted.
2. Add butter in small pieces, stirring continuously. Remove from heat.
3. Whisk egg yolks and sugar in a bowl until pale and thick. Add vanilla essence and brandy or Van der Hum.
4. Add egg mix to chocolate and beat for about 2 minutes until blended.
5. Whisk egg whites until stiff and fold into chocolate mix together with cream. Pour into a glass bowl and chill for about 8 hours. Garnish with grated chocolate.

Variation
Substitute dark chocolate with white chocolate, and brandy with Cape Velvet liqueur.

PEACH YOGHURT PUDDING
Simple and basic is sometimes the best!

SERVES 6–8

2 x 80 g peach jellies
125 ml (½ cup) boiling water
410 g can evaporated milk, chilled
500 ml (2 cups) peach and granadilla yoghurt

1. Dissolve the jellies in boiling water and leave to cool slightly.
2. Beat chilled evaporated milk until foamy. Stir in dissolved jelly and yoghurt.
3. Refrigerate for 4–6 hours until set.

BUTTERMILK PUDDING
Delicious, with a light and fluffy texture.

SERVES 6

125 g butter
200 ml (¾ cup) sugar
2 eggs
250 ml (1 cup) cake flour
7 ml (1¼ tsp) baking powder
2 ml (¼ tsp) salt
500 ml (2 cups) buttermilk
125 ml (½ cup) milk

1. Preheat oven to 160 °C (325 °F).
2. Cream butter and sugar.
3. Add eggs one at a time, beating well after each one.
4. Sift dry ingredients together and add to butter mixture together with milk and buttermilk.
5. Pour batter into a greased medium-sized ovenproof dish and bake for 45–60 minutes, depending on depth of dish. Serve hot with apricot jam.

LAYERED FRUIT SALAD

SERVES 4–6

1 large pawpaw or melon
250 g strawberries, halved
2 oranges, cut in wedges
4 guavas or kiwi fruits, sliced
30 black grapes, pitted and halved
115 g can granadilla pulp

DRESSING
30 ml (2 tbsp) chopped fresh mint
30 ml (2 tbsp) fresh lemon juice
60 ml (¼ cup) fresh orange juice
15 ml (1 tbsp) honey

1. Peel pawpaw and cut in half. Scoop out seeds. Cut flesh in long strips.
2. Top with strawberries and other fruit, layering each.
3. For dressing: Combine ingredients and pour over fruit.

CRÊPE SUZETTE

MAKES ABOUT 15

250 ml (1 cup) cake flour
2 ml (¼ tsp) salt
2 eggs
150 ml water
± 200 ml (¾ cup) milk

SAUCE

60 ml (¼ cup) brown sugar
50 g butter
125 ml (½ cup) fresh orange juice
15 ml (1 tbsp) orange rind
10 ml (2 tsp) cornflour
30 ml (2 tbsp) water
80 ml (⅓ cup) brandy

1. Sift flour and salt together. Whisk eggs with water and add to flour with enough milk to make a thin batter.
2. Leave to stand for at least 1 hour.
3. Lightly oil a heavy-based frying pan and heat. Pour batter into pan to just cover the base and fry until lightly browned on both sides. Fold pancake into quarters and set aside. Continue making pancakes until all the batter is used up.
4. For sauce: Melt sugar and butter. Add orange juice and rind and simmer until sugar is completely dissolved. Mix cornflour in water and thicken sauce slightly. Add pancakes to sauce and heat through.
5. Warm brandy, pour over pancakes and ignite. Serve when flames die down.

FROM LEFT TO RIGHT: *Layered Fruit Salad, Peach Yoghurt Pudding (see page 108).*

FRUIT TRIFLE

SERVES 6–8

80 g (1 pkt) lime jelly
300 g vanilla sponge cake
80 ml (⅓ cup) smooth apricot jam
60 ml (¼ cup) medium cream sherry
410 g can sliced peaches, drained
750 ml (3 cups) fresh vanilla custard
250 ml (1 cup) fresh cream, whipped
glacé cherries and whipped cream to garnish

1. Dissolve jelly in 375 ml (1½ cups) boiling water. Add 375 ml (1½ cups) cold water. Leave to set overnight. Cut into cubes.
2. Cut cake into 7 cm thick slices. Spread with smooth apricot jam.
3. Using a 23 x 23 cm dish, layer base with half the sponge cake. Sprinkle the cake with sherry.
4. Place a layer of peaches on top of sponge cake, followed by half the jelly and half the custard and cream. Repeat with all remaining ingredients.
5. Garnish with cherries and cream.

VANILLA MOUSSE

SERVES 6

1 litre (4 cups) milk
4 eggs, separated
125 ml (½ cup) sugar
30 ml (2 tbsp) gelatine
60 ml (¼ cup) cold water
5 ml (1 tsp) vanilla essence
fresh fruit to garnish

1. Heat milk, but do not boil.
2. Beat egg yolks and sugar. Add hot milk gradually and return to heat. Cook for 1 minute. Remove from heat.
3. Soak gelatine in cold water for a few minutes. Dissolve over hot water. Add gelatine and vanilla essence to egg mixture.
4. Beat egg whites until stiff and fold into mixture. (It will look curdled.)
5. Rinse a large mould with cold water. Pour in mixture and leave to set in refrigerator for a few hours.
6. Dip mould gently in hot water and turn out to serve. Garnish with any fresh fruit in season.

Vanilla Mousse

index

a
accompaniments 90–103
almonds, toasting 107
angel fish with mustard baste 66
apricot glaze 23
aromatics 11
askoek 93
asparagus and potato chip crisp 31
aubergine 96

b
bacon pastry twists 31
balsamic vinegar 103
balsamic, garlic and herb dressing 103
bananas, bacon-wrapped 28
　flambéed 107
　grilled 106
barbecue marinade 21
　sauce 35
basic marinade with wine 21
basil 60
bastes 22
　fruit 22
　mustard 66
　red wine 36
　rosemary 22
　wine 22
bay leaves 58
beef and veal 32–41
beef patties (burgers) 35
beef rib roll, spit-roast 88
beer marinade 21
beer marinated steak 32
boerewors (traditional sausage) 39
braai methods
　gas or electric 8
　kettle braai 6–8
　potjie 11
　smoking 11
　wood or charcoal 6
bran 90
bread and butter pudding 106
breadcrumbs 53

breads 90–95
　cheese and sun-dried tomato 92
　fruit health 90
　mealie 93
　toast 94
broccoli salad 103
burgers (*see* beef patties)
buttermilk pudding 108
butters, savoury 93

c
calamari in garlic 66
carpetbag steak 40
celery 78
charcoal braai (*see* wood or charcoal braai)
cheese and sun-dried tomato bread 92
cheese slices, savoury 27
cheesy rolls, chutney 26
chicken liver pâté 24
chicken, barbecue 75
　breasts, smoked (kettle braai only) 75
　curry, potjie 82
　in garlic, grilled sesame 74
　kebabs, sweet-and-sour 71
　lemon-pepper spatchcock 68
　parmesan 72
　peri-peri spatchcock 74
　roast (kettle braai only) 71
　satays with peanut sauce 31
　stuffed sun-dried tomato 68
　tropical honey 72
　upside-down, potjie 76
　wings, barbecued 28
　with mayonnaise, flamed 75
chillies 74
chipolatas with mayonnaise chutney 28
chives 75
chocolate mousse, superb 108
chops, barbecue 45
coconut milk, making 31
cooking methods 10
　hints for meat braais 17
　hints for fish braais 67
cooking times 10

coriander 46, 82
corn on the cob 99
crayfish, grilled 67
crêpe suzette 109
cumin 46
curry offal, potjie 85

d
desserts 104–110
dill 63
dips 27
　avocado, creamy 27
　pineapple 27
　tuna 27
dressings 100–103
　balsamic, garlic and herb 103
　mustard and honey 103
　pineapple 24
　yoghurt, creamy 102
duck, roast with orange and ginger (kettle braai only) 70
dumplings, herb 78
　spicy 106

e
eisbein with dried fruit, potjie 81

f
fennel 66
fillet with chilli sauce 40
fish and seafood 60–67
fish in banana leaves 60
fruit, baste 22
　kebabs with pineapple dressing 24
　salad, layered 108
fuels 8
　charcoal and briquettes 8
　coals 8
　firelighter fluid 8
　firelighters 8
　wood 8

g
gammon steaks with apricot glaze 51
garlic 50
　over coals 99
gas or electric braai 8

ginger 42
glazes 23
　apricot 23
　honey 23
　honey and orange 60
　pineapple 23
grid care 10

h
hake in foil 67
honey and orange glaze 60
honey glaze 23

k
kabeljou (kob), grilled with cashew nut filling 63
kebabs, ginger-flavoured 42
　with pineapple dressing, fruit 24
　with red wine baste, steak 36
kettle braai (Weber) 6, 8
　direct cooking method 8
　indirect cooking method 8
kingklip with sun-dried tomato marinade 64
koftas, date and almond 28
krummelpap 94

l
lamb, and pumpkin pot (potjie) 85
　chops, honey and chutney 49
　citrus 48
　cutlets with roasted red pepper sauce 42
　oriental leg of 49
　rib, coriander 46
　riblets, glazed 47
　shoulder blade with rosemary baste 48
　with caramelized onions 46
　with dumplings, tomato potjie 78
　with lemon and mint 44
larding 81
leeks 76
lemon and herb marinade 21
lentils 102

m

malva pudding 104
marinades 18–21
   barbecue 21
   basic with wine 21
   beer 21
   containers 18
   ingredients 18
   key points 18
   lemon and herb 21
   spicy oriental 21
   sun-dried tomato 64
   yoghurt 21
marjoram 72
marscarpone cheese 104
marshmallows over the coals 106
mealie bread 93
mealie meal porridge 94
meat 32–59
   beef 12
     cuts 15
   choosing 10
   fish 14
   lamb 12
     cuts 16
   pork 12
     cuts 16
   poultry 13–14
   venison 12–13
     cuts 17
meatballs wrapped in bacon, spicy 28
melba toast 27
mushroom sauce, creamy 35
mustard 75
   and honey dressing 103
   baste 66
mutton
   chops with tomato and thyme 49
   chops, tandoori 46
mutton and lamb 42–49

n

noisettes 45

o

olive oil 68
ostrich, potjie with sweet potatoes 85
   steaks 72
oxtail, delicious potjie 78

p

pap tart, savoury 94
paprika chicken, spit-roast 88
parsley 49
pasta salad with olives and sun-dried tomatoes 103
pâté, smoked 27
peach yoghurt pudding 108
peppercorns, green 32
pepper-origanum steaks 38
pesto sauce 36
   steak 36
pineapple glaze 23
pizza, Mediterranean 90
pork 50–57
   chops, with pineapple and ginger 56
     delicious sage 54
     dried fruit stuffed 53
     smoked with mango 56
   fillet, for salad 51
     honey-glazed 57
   kebabs with peppadews 54
   neck roll, spit-roast 89
   pin wheels 54
   rashers with garlic and rosemary baste 50
   rib chops with avocado sauce 56
   roast (for kettle braai only) 53
   sausages wrapped in bacon 57
   spare ribs, with peach sauce 53
     barbecue 50
porterhouse steak with mustard-sherry sauce 41
potato and mushroom bake 99
potato salad with hot bacon dressing 100
potatoes with soup powder, easy 98
   with sour cream and chives, jacket 98
potbrood, honey 95
potjies 11, 76–85
   ingredients 11
   tips 11
poultry 68–75
prawn, kebabs with mint and parmesan cheese 64
peri-peri 26
preparing a fire 8
pumpkin, stuffed 99

r

red wine baste 36
rice, curred brown and lentil salad 102
roast in coals, salt-crust 40
roosterkoek 93
rosemary 48
   baste 22
rubs 23
rump steak with lemon-garlic butter 36

s

sage 54
salads and dressings 100–103
salmon steaks with basil 60
sardines, grilled 64
sauces, avocado 56
   barbecue 35
   chilli 40
   green peppercorn 32
   litchi 39
   mushroom, creamy 35
   mustard-sherry 41
   peach 53
   peanut 31
   pesto 36
   roasted red pepper 42
   sherry 39
   tartare 66
sausage on a skewer, spiral 44
seafood pot with rice, potjie 82
sesame seeds 74
short rib with cola 40
smoking 11
   sawdust 11
snacks 24–31
snoek, grilled with apricot baste 67
sole in creamy mushroom sauce 66
sosaties, traditional 45
soya sauce 50
spicy oriental marinade 21
spinach salad 100
spit-roast 86–89
   methods 86–88
steak, beer marinated 32
   carpetbag 40
   gammon steaks with apricot glaze 51
   kebabs with red wine baste 36
   ostrich steaks 72
   pepper-origanum 38
   pesto 36
   porterhouse steak with mustard-sherry sauce 41
   rump steak with lemon-garlic butter 36
   salmon steaks with basil 60
   T-bone with green peppercorn sauce 32
   venison steaks, buttermilk 58
stir-fry with pasta 48
stokbrood 93
stuffing, thyme 88
stywe pap 94
sun-dried tomato marinade 64
sun-dried tomatoes 68
sweet peppers 62
sweet potato in coals 96
   with rosemary, potjie 81
sweet-and-sour onions 101

t

tartare sauce 66
T-bone with green peppercorn sauce 32
temperature control 9
three-bean salad with basil 102
thyme 49
tiramisu 104
toast breads 94
trifle, fruit 110
trout, orange and dill 63
trussing 88
tuna and pepper kebabs 62
turkey drumsticks 71
turmeric 45

u

utensils 10

v

vanilla 106
   mousse 110
veal in sherry sauce 39
   kebabs with litchi sauce, concertina 39
vegetables 96–99
   char-grilled 96
   kebabs 96
   marinated 102
   parcels in foil 96
   pot, mixed potjie 76
venison 58–59
   fine shredded 58
   leg in red wine potjie 81
   potjie 79
   saddle with wine baste (for kettle braai only) 58
   sausage 59
   steaks, buttermilk 58

w

wine baste 22
wood or charcoal braai
   barrel 6
   built-in 6
   disposable 6
   kettle braai (Weber) 6
   upright open 6

y

yellowtail, grilled with rosemary baste 64
yoghurt dressing, creamy 102
   marinade 21